HOW

TRAIN

YOUR PUPPY

FOR KIDS

STEP-BY-STEP TRAINING GUIDE, TIPS, AND TRICKS TO
RAISE YOUR PUPPY IN FUN AND EASY WAYS

ANDREW MALCOM

TABLE OF CONTENTS

A SPECIAL GIFT TO OUR READERS!

Included with your purchase of this book is our **5 Step Challenge** on how to train your dog to roll over. This is a great way to show all your friends and family a neat little trick your fur ball can do.

Included in your 5 Step Challenge is a **checklist** of the most essential things you need for your puppy before it arrives.

Use the Link:
Andrewmalcom.com

Or Scan the QR Code

JOIN OUR ONLINE SUPPORT GROUP

To maximize the value of your training, I highly encourage you to join our tight-knit community on Facebook, where you will be able to ask questions and get tips and tricks.

Use the link:
https://www.facebook.com/groups/puppytrainingcommunity

Or Scan the QR Code

INTRODUCTION

Your family has decided to adopt a fur friend! Imagine this situation. One day, you return home and see the whole house is a mess, the furniture is in shreds, and there's dog pee on the rug. How shocked will you be? Wouldn't it be natural to think, "Puppies aren't supposed to be dirty; they're just supposed to be cute."

Well, of course, they are supposed to be cute. But, they are living things with their behaviors and own ways of thinking. How will they know what is right and what is wrong unless you train them?

FOR THE PARENTS

You may be thinking about why you should involve your children in training the family puppy. The American Kennel Club states that consistency is vital for training dogs. If you do not include your kids in this process from an early age, your dog will not recognize them as a family member. I knew a family who wouldn't involve their kids in obedience training, and the dog grew up aloof from them. The more you get your child involved with the puppy, the more you will connect as a family.

Keeping your kids away from the family puppy is also potentially impossible. You live in the same house. The wholesome approach would help each side develop a healthy relationship based on mutual respect and adoration. This way, children learn that pets have emotions. So, while you teach your kids that tails are not toys, you also teach them positive ways to involve your puppy. In return, your puppy becomes a quintessential household pet. After all, raising a puppy isn't much different from raising a child.

Involving the family ensures that they grow up in a loving environment feeling safe and happy.

FOR THE KiDS!

You are the stars of my book. I hope it will be a key to a world of adventure for you and your fur friend.

So, you've decided to bring a new puppy into the family. That's great news! Adopting a dog and making them a part of the family is a big step to take, and you probably think you're ready for it. You may be surprised to hear that you're not as prepared as you think.

I thought I was ready the first time I brought a dog home with me (after months of begging my parents), but boy, was I mistaken.

I was so happy knowing that my dog and I would be best friends. I would play with him and feed him good food every night. When I finally got him home, I realized it was a lot more complicated than that.

My puppy made a mess everywhere he went. He wasn't house trained, so he peed all over the floor. He even bit my furniture. Sometimes, he would growl at me when I tried to feed him. He was very disobedient and wouldn't listen to a single thing I said. He even bit me when I was trying to put his collar on. I only realized then how unprepared I was. Of course, when I understood this, I decided to train my puppy.

When I began training Hector (my puppy), I was not much older than you. I found that the more I actively engaged him, the more I learned. In return, Hector slowly learned to obey all of my commands. We grew up as best friends from this day on. He would wait for me to come back from school every evening. We would train together for an hour after that, and it was the best hour of my day. When you are older, you, too, will look back on this time spent training your puppy and smile.

Having a dog in your life is great. There are many benefits and rewards to reap from it, but it is a lot of hard work. It takes dedication and time to train your dog, but this will help give them a happy life. You're reading this book that shows that you have the love and dedication to get through these challenging times.

HOW CAN I HELP?

You may be thinking, how can this man, who I hardly know, help me? Since my childhood, I've grown up loving and training many dogs. I've gone on to train other dogs and give their owners the key to a happy family with an obedient house-pet. I know it's hard to do, but when you see how close you and your puppy will become because of this training, imagine how proud you will feel.

Take my word for it. After training dogs and teaching dog owners for many years, all the hard work is worth it in the end.

Don't be discouraged if things get rough down the road. That means you're getting closer to having a fully trained and happy member of the family. Get ready for a life filled with constant companionship, long days playing outside, wagging tails, kisses, and a best friend who will always be there for you. That's what it means to have a fully trained dog in your life.

What you are about to learn will amaze you! I will teach you to train your puppy so that they will learn how to interact with you and other animals. They'll be taught good manners and become obedient. Most importantly, a stronger bond will be created between you and your dog when you train them properly. A dog that the whole family trains are more likely to see itself as a family member. They will live a longer, safer, and happier life.

A family pet needs involvement from the entire family. If only your parents train the puppy, it will only see them as its family and follow only their instructions. Therefore, you need to be involved in your puppy training process to know that you're part of the family. That's why you should try as much as possible to participate in the training process. Don't just let your parents do all the work while you only play.

The initial phase can be challenging, and it's a lot of responsibility. It takes dedication and love, but I know you have it in you. You're seeking help from this book, so I know you're willing to put the work in and train your dog properly.

As we move ahead, we will uncover all the secrets to helping you connect with your puppy. By reading this book, you will feel happy and confident with your puppy. This is the key to learning from my book.

You and your puppy will develop a secret language, and imagine how much fun you will have together. Imagine you are sitting in a big crowded room, and you and your puppy are talking to each other in your code. The bond will be extraordinary.

The first step begins with understanding that we need to learn more to do better. Let's say you love painting and you want to be an artist. So, you will take some time to paint and get better at it every day, right? You will watch tutorials, learn new tricks, and take advice and guidance from trained professionals. In the same way, consider this book as a key. It will open the door to new knowledge for you. I am excited for you to learn with me.

Welcome to a great future for your puppy and you!

1

WOW! YOU'RE GETTING A PUPPY!

If you have decided to get a fur-ball puppy home, you already know that you are in for a ride. Everything feels sunnier with a dog by your side. But did you know that the time of the year and your routine are both crucial things to consider before you get a sweet puppy? Let's talk about some tips and tricks to help you find the perfect time for bringing your ball of joy home.

WHAT IS THE BEST TiME TO BRiNG MY PUPPY HOME?

Several factors will determine the best time to bring your puppy home. Let's have a look at them.

- The right time slot will ensure your puppy has a wholesome and attention-filled environment to grow up in. For example, you may think that holidays like Christmas are an excellent time for a fur-friend. But be wary.

- Holidays are hectic for all of us. We spend a lot of time with our friends and family, and many people are in the house. You know and love these people, but your puppy will not know any of them. This can be too scary for them, and they may show signs of aggression or simply hide.

- During holidays, you will also be occupied with festivities and not have any time to give to your puppy. This means you will miss out on their initial developmental phase, which means your puppy will feel sad and neglected. After all, it is a baby. How would you feel if your parents left you alone in a crowded room full of strangers? Lonely and upset, right? It's the same for them.

- Festivities are also a time for unwrapping presents, and this may mean our houses are more messed up. Your puppy won't know the difference between dog food and wrapping paper and may eat something potentially dangerous. Puppies are often naughty, and they try to get their human's attention by doing silly things like chewing on furniture or paper, eating things they shouldn't, and getting into all kinds of trouble. So, you have to be the grown-up and take care of them.

- Winter, and any other time of the year when there are fireworks, can upset your puppy. Dogs are very sensitive to noise. Did you know they can even hear things humans can't? So, imagine how painful the sound of loud firecrackers will be for them. It will be scarier if you are busy with friends and family and cannot be there to comfort them.

- If you live in a cold or rainy city, it will be harder to housebreak your puppy in the winter or rainy seasons. The outdoors can be very scary for new eyes, and if the weather is also bad, why would the puppy want to leave the comfort of your home?

- In comparison, spring and summer are much better months. Spring can still be harsh, but late spring brings with it the perfect dog-walking season. Long sunny days, lesser chaos of festivities, school vacations, ideal weather for outdoor activities- all of these conditions are optimal for when you want to bring your puppy home.

- Housebreaking is easier in the warm months because your puppy will *want* to explore the outdoors. So, not only will they learn better, you will have more time to spend on them.

The next important thing is your schedule. You have to ensure that you don't have too many engagements when deciding to get a puppy. You want to be involved in training them, in getting them to know and love you. The best way to succeed in this is to be involved with them from their babyhood. So, consider these factors beforehand.

- Do you have any holidays ahead? And, not the busy ones where all your time is spent with other people. Can you make time for bonding with your puppy without having to worry about missing other things?

- Are your parents working late shifts? If yes, will there be someone to take care of your puppy when your parents and you are not home? Puppies love socializing and being the center of attention. Leaving them alone in a house for too long may make them upset. If they get upset or bored, they become destructive, so you have to ensure that they deserve attention.

- Finally, what do you see for your puppy and yourself? Do you have any big plans for the two of you? Will you always be around for them? A puppy is a wonderful friend and a commitment. When you bring them home, it is as good as opening yourself to a world of love. They will love you unconditionally. So, make sure to bring them home at a time when you will be able to return that love. This will not only make your puppy love you more, but it will also give you a friend for life.

QUALITIES TO LOOK FOR WHEN GETTING A PUPPY

The season is perfect! You cannot wait to bring your little friend home and begin training them. Have you thought about what your puppy should be like? There's a saying in the English language- *"birds of a feather flock together."* It means that two living beings of the exact nature have the highest possibility of being friends. So, before you prepare your heart and home, also think of the qualities you want your puppy to have.

- Your lifestyle plays a significant role. Are you active? Do you enjoy sports or outdoor activities? Would you like to spend many hours with your dog in the yard, playing and training them? Then, a high-energy breed like a golden retriever would make an excellent companion for

Golden Retriever

you. Some dogs have higher energy needs than others and will do better with high-energy companions.

- On the other hand, if you enjoy being at home more and cannot imagine a better life than snuggling on the sofa with your fur-friend, breeds like Basset Hounds would be the perfect fit. Basset Hounds love to sleep and snuggle all day, and if that is what you like too, imagine how much fun you will have together.

Basset Hound

- Next, do you want a pure-bred or a mixed-breed puppy? Mixed-breed puppies may have a lower risk of birth defects (diseases inherited from parents). But, it may also be challenging to find out their parent lines. If you want to know both parents and your dog's birth history, a pure breed is a great option. This will also help you understand what kind of dog your puppy will grow into. Say you get a mixed-breed thinking it will grow into a small homely dog, but it grows up big and highly energetic. This is a crucial point to consider (*Mixed or Purebred Puppy: Which Is Better?*, 2017).

Husky

- Do you want a fluffy, furry friend? If your answer is yes, then be prepared for lots of shedding. Puppies with extra fur can shed all year round. They also need cooler climates to thrive in. Huskies, Malamutes, Golden Retrievers, and Samoyeds are some breeds that shed seasonally and have very high grooming needs. So, if you want that extra fur on your little friend, be prepared to brush and groom them. This will increase bonding between the two of you, and your puppy will learn to trust you more.

Samoyed

- Is your home big or a cozy apartment? Based on your living area, you can get a puppy who will grow up to become a big dog, or you can go for small apartment dogs like Dachshunds, Chihuahuas, and Corgis. Dachshunds and Corgis are perfect if you want a small dog with a big personality.

Chihuahua

Dachshund

Corgi

- What would you want your puppy's nature to be like? Would you like them to be quiet, shy, or independent? Breeds like Huskies, Greyhounds, and Dalmatians are shy and independent. Or, would you want them to be social, friendly, and all over your face all the time? Breeds such as Golden Retrievers love being with their humans and socializing. They thrive when you have friends over, and they'll probably want to get to know all of them. Some breeds are also more curious than others, and you'll find them up to all kinds of mischief. Are you playing a game? They must understand it. Are you reading a book? They will want to taste it. Breeds like Boxers and Beagles have a very playful, curious personality.

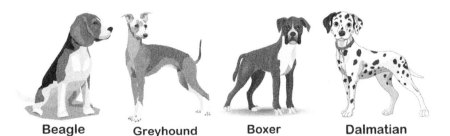

Beagle   **Greyhound**   **Boxer**   **Dalmatian**

- Finally, consider all the health requirements of your puppy. Some dogs need more maintenance than others. For example, Golden Retrievers need a lot of skincare. So, the more high maintenance your puppy is, the more you will need to book appointments with pet salons and pet care facilities. There will also be varieties of dog food for different breeds, supplements, and bone and joint care tonics. Who doesn't enjoy the idea of a soft, furry baby nestled in our arms? That comes with commitments, so be ready for those (*Dog Temperament Types*, 2020).

As always, the best fit is different for different families. It would be a good idea to involve your parents in the process of choosing a puppy. You can list the qualities you would like them to have and go to them with this list. They can then take you to meet the parents of your forever friend and help you begin your incredible journey with them.

WHAT TO AVOID WHEN CHOOSING A PUPPY

You've decided that your house feels empty without the pitter-patter of furry paws. Most of your free time is spent looking at pictures of puppies, and you are constantly daydreaming about having one of your own. You get excited whenever you see puppies outdoors and cannot wait for the time to come when you can get one home with you. You've even got a name ready for when they arrive.

Having a puppy will surely fill up the empty spaces in your heart and home. They are like the sweetest medicine, adding laughter and joy to our lives. However, there are some things you should be mindful of when choosing your little friend.

- Don't take two puppies simultaneously if you aren't ready. Two puppies will mean double the responsibilities. You will have to train them equally, clean up after them, be responsible for breaking fights between the two, and always be one step ahead of them. Puppies are naughty creatures. That's not a bad thing, though. It simply means they will look for ways to keep getting your attention. When one does it, it's adorable. But think of how tired you will be if two of them are constantly keeping you on your feet. Unless you feel you can take that on, it may be best to get one puppy.

- Don't impulse-buy your puppy. It happens to all of us. We go to a dog center, get overwhelmed by the cuteness, and take the first puppy that appeals to us. It's like taking candy with perfect packaging, but once you open and try it, you find it doesn't suit your taste buds. Do some studying on different dog breeds, their qualities, exercise, and health requirements. When you study, you will find a puppy suited to your nature. This will ensure that you develop a strong friendship with them, based on similar likes and dislikes.

- Don't bring your puppy home if there is a lot of disturbance. For example, if you are changing houses, or your house is being repaired or renovated, or have house-guests over. Puppies will thrive better in a peaceful abode where you will have all your attention on them. If you move houses, you will have to re-train your puppy and housebreak them from the beginning. That will be double the work and no fun.

- Remember that white and light-colored dogs will need a lot of grooming. They get dirty easily, and a little bit of dust can settle on their skin and make them look untidy. If you want a low-maintenance puppy, go for deeper-colored ones.

- Invest in your puppy before they come home. It's a bad idea to bring them to a home where there is nothing for them. Remember your first few months in this world? Didn't your parents have toys and cots ready for you? Was your house baby-proofed? These little puppies make us feel like we belong. So, before your puppy comes home, prepare your living space. Get dog toys, training toys, and some interactive games for your fur friend. You can invest in a crate if you want to crate-train them. Get some soft towels and dog shampoo for giving them baths. Make sure you have puppy food and supplements. You can even get a small dog bed for them to nap in. Make your house a home for your puppy.

- Finally, please make sure everyone in your home is aware of a new friend coming into all your life. Don't get the puppy from a friend and surprise everyone because *you need to be involved in loving and caring for them.* It's a team effort.

These guidelines helped me when I was choosing a puppy. I realized that I had to get one that would fit into a medium-sized apartment, wouldn't shed a lot, and be of an easy-going temperament. Because I knew what type of puppy I wanted, I got one that matched my needs to the tee. Years later, we are inseparable.

PREPARING YOUR HOME

By now, you already know that your puppy will be like a baby. I told you that when a baby comes into a home, we take some time to prepare the house for their arrival. This isn't just a way of making them feel welcome; it's also a means to develop a bond with them. Just think, when you started living in your home, if there would have been no toys, or your favorite food, or a place for you to sleep in. Would you have liked that? It's the same for puppies. When you bring them into a prepared home, they feel they are in a safe environment *that has been made for them*. They begin looking at your apartment as a territory where they can peacefully live and bond with you. Below are some of the steps you can take to ensure your puppy feels welcomed.

- To start with, get enough supplies. I've mentioned what you may need in the last section.

- You can consider keeping a temporary designated space for your puppy. This will be the *puppy zone* in your house, where the training can take place. You can ward off this area with baby-gates for those times when your puppy is being extra naughty and needs a few minutes in the corner. When you are busy with work, this is an appropriate way to make sure your puppy is safe and isn't getting into any trouble.

- School and work can keep all family members busy. So, before you bring your puppy home, consider day-care or hiring someone to watch your puppy. This is especially important when your puppy is in the training stage. Being left alone for too long will make them feel lonely and destructive, and they can damage your belongings.

- Consider taking a safety check of your house. Anything that your puppy can smell and chew, it will attempt to. It's not alarming; instead, it's a way for your puppy to familiarize themselves with your home. Think of what may potentially harm a small fur-ball. Jagged edges, leaving floor cleaners around, or anything with chemicals/substances that will harm your puppy should be kept out of their reach.

Finally, before you go to get your little friend, keep a vet's number stuck on the fridge or wherever you keep emergency notes. Puppies have a high trouble quotient, which means they are always doing things they shouldn't. It's just like taking on a child and teaching them to live in society. So, the more prepared you are, the more harmonious your co-existence will be.

ESSENTIAL EQUIPMENT TO MAKE YOUR PUPPY FEEL AT HOME

Your mind is made up, the day is almost here, and you are so excited to bring your new friend home. But, let us take a minute to go over what essentials you will need to make your home a home for them too.

- A home isn't one without a comfortable bed. You may want your puppy to sleep with you, but buy a bed for them just in case. They should have their zone in the  house. You can go for *Vetbeds,* which are snug, durable, and equipped with good drainage properties (if your wee buddy has a minor accident at night, and this is common when they are just housebroken). You can get a stretchable one if your puppy grows into a big dog. And since puppies are little chew-maniacs, give preference to comfort and durability over the physical appeal.

- You will need a couple of bowls and a designated feeding place with a stand (for tall breeds). The bowls for food and water should be separate. Keep a few extra so that you can alternate and make it fun for both your puppy and you. Here's a strange thing- my puppy would only eat from plates. No matter how much we tried, she preferred her meals on dishes like us humans! Be prepared for such surprises too. It's part of the fun- imagine all the new things you'll be learning.

- Getting a crate is one of the most important things you will do for your puppy. Never associate the crate with punishment time because they will begin to hate it. Rather, make the crate a place of love and safety. Add a few cute plushies, a soft blanket, and a few

chew toys, and let your puppy associate the crate as a home within a home. Remove their collars before entering the crate to avoid them getting stuck to anything. And don't crate them for too long in the day because they will feel neglected.

- Some dogs like having four-poster beds, which help keep them safe and out of trouble if they have to be alone. If you get one, make sure it fits your puppy snugly so that they don't feel like you are trying to restrict them.

- If you live in a cooler climate and want a small dog like a chihuahua, consider getting some clothes for them. It will keep them snug when they have to train outdoors. A raincoat is helpful for monsoon walks too. They don't have to wear clothes in the apartment, though.

- Getting a collar is so much fun. I got my puppy a collar customized with her name, birthday, and emergency contact. I chose an adjustable buckle because she grew so fast. This is very important. Get a size suitable for the  breed. It shouldn't be so tight that you cannot slip two fingers in, nor so loose that it can slip over your puppy's head. You can also get a body harness once they are leash-trained. Body harnesses are snug and pretty, and there are so many varieties.

- If you want to train your puppy to travel in a car, get a dog guard and secure it with the car seat harness. Alternatively, you can get a crate or a car cage. This will give your puppy their space and also allow them to be safe and comfortable. Try short trips at first, checking to see if they make your puppy car-sick. In case they do get sick, consider alternative options like keeping windows down or adjusting their seating area. Typically, back seats are likelier to cause nausea as the car sways more at the back.

- In some countries, you must inscribe your name and address on your dog's collar. I wholeheartedly encourage you to do this. It will ensure complete safety for your puppy. Remember when you were kids and just starting at school? Did your parents make name tags for you and attach them to your uniforms/bags/tiffins? My parents did this all the time, and looking back, I'm glad they did. It gave me a sense of identity. You will be your puppy's whole world. Let everyone else know that.

- Consider getting a microchip for your puppy. This is a safety measure that you will hopefully never need to rely upon- but it is always better to be safe than sorry. Some quotes never go old, and this is one of them. If your puppy ever gets lost, the microchip is a guarantee that it will find its way back to you.

- Get a nice, strong lead for your puppy, depending on their size and breed. Don't go for something too short or too long. It should feel comfortable in your hands. Test it out by taking a trial walk. Whichever type you choose, attach the lead to the collar's *'D-Ring'* and not the split ring. The latter connects to your dog's identity tag and isn't strong enough to endure the weight of your dog.

- Get plenty of toys for your puppy. Playing with them is one of the most joyful bonding experiences, and more toys mean varied play. You can get tug-of-war toys, balls, boomerangs, chew-bones, durable plushies- the options are endless.

- You can get an anti-pulling aid to stop your puppy from pulling the leash too hard during walks but do be cautious. Many of them are designed to hurt your puppy, and they are not tolerated well. Ask around, and make sure your puppy feels comfortable with the aid.

- Get poo-bags and picking aids to help you clean up after your puppy. This may be unpleasant initially, but it's a natural and normal function of most living things.

- Puppies are such beautiful creatures, and to maintain their health, they need to be groomed regularly. Get a rubber-toothed or short-bristled brush for your puppy.

- At home, always be gentle and slow when brushing your pup. This is a tender bonding moment between the two of you and will help you build trust. Puppies need to have their nails trimmed if they get too long. Invest in a good nail trimmer for this purpose. Finally, some dogs' coats can burn if left in the sun for too long, so you can get a dog-friendly sun cream, especially if your dog has a white coat or little fur on them.

- Get a gentle, dog-friendly shampoo. Dogs don't require more than one bath a month, so invest in a good shampoo. Some dogs love the water; others can be more stubborn. Make it playtime for both of you.

- Did you know dogs get gum disease? So, to prevent that, brush your puppy's teeth with a dog-friendly toothpaste and toothbrush. It will pay off later.

INTRODUCING YOUR PUPPY TO YOUR HOME

Now that you've decided upon which puppy you'll get, it's time to prepare them for the grand homecoming. Some things can be done to ensure this is easy for your puppy and you. Remember that your puppy will enter a new world, where everything is unfamiliar to them (Stregowski, 2020). It's normal for some of them to feel anxious and overwhelmed. On the other hand, some puppies fit into their new homes like pieces of a puzzle. We all want this to happen, so what can we do?

- Choose a spot where you would like to begin your puppy's potty training. This is housebreaking, and you need to do it if you don't want a house full of poop and pee in random places. Choose a command to potty-train your puppy, like "go potty" or "good potty." Don't be uncomfortable because this is a natural part of getting your puppy to know its proper spots. Whenever they follow your instructions, praise and reward them. In time, they will associate *going to the potty* in the designated place as good behavior.

- Introduce them to the home gradually. If you live in a multiple-storeyed home, go one floor at a time. Taking the stairs can be potentially dangerous before your puppy is used to climbing them. So you may want to begin by cordoning off the upper floors and making them familiar with the ground floor first.

- Don't let them explore the house willy-nilly. It's too much *sensory overload.* Imagine you are in Willy Wonka's Chocolate Factory, and the Oompa-Loompas leave you unsupervised. You'll be overwhelmed and probably eat too much chocolate and fall sick. For your puppy, the new home is nothing short of the Chocolate Factory, a wonderful, new place full of new smells and sights. Begin with a small area, like their crate or their food and water zones. Then, introduce them to the rest of the house bit by bit.

- Take some time out to introduce each of the family members to your puppy. This will be a very exciting phase, and all of you may want to cuddle them and pass them around. But, rather than doing that, go one by one. Let the puppy smell each of you, feel you with their paws and nose, identify a smell with you. This smell will help them differentiate between their families and other people.

- Puppies are terrible chewers. They have a nipping phase when they like to bite everything. Make sure you have enough chewy toys to keep their boredom at bay, or else you can wish the ends of your sofas and your soft toys goodbye.

- Finally, show your puppy their sleeping space. Puppies can sleep between 15-20 hours a day. They may just drop while playing with you and doze off. But, if this happens, pick them up and place them in their designated sleeping zone. Don't think of it as a puppy jail. Instead, it's a safe space for them to retire to when they want to sleep, just like you have your bedrooms to sleep in (Reisen, 2020).

With enough encouragement, your puppy will become familiar with the house in no time. Everyone faces some hiccups at the beginning. Don't let that discourage you because I promise that you will do a great job.

 **KEY POiNTS**

Well done for coming this far. You now know enough to bring a little puppy home with you. Before we move into the next chapter, here's a quick summary of what we just read.

- Be mindful of the time when you are getting a puppy. Your house should not be too busy or be full of guests constantly. It's best to get a puppy around spring or summer when the festive season is over, and you have more quiet time to train them.

- Make a list of essential qualities before choosing a puppy. There are no two dog breeds that are the same, and they all have their little quirks. The temperament of the puppy should ideally match yours. So, if you love sports and outdoor activities, get an active, sporty puppy! And if you are more fond of your room and your bed, get a quiet, homely breed.

- Make sure everyone in your home is on the same page as you. Raising the puppy is a team effort, and the more love, the healthier they will grow up to become. Also, don't get two puppies together if you don't have previous experience. Don't get one out of an impulse because it's a choice that won't just change your life, but theirs too.

- Prepare your home for your puppy. Make sure there are enough supplies; that way, your puppy will always be taken care of. Remember to not leave your puppy alone for too long, especially not in the training phase.

- Introduce your puppy to your home gradually. Taking all of it in together on the first day will lead to an overload of the senses. Mark off their feeding area, show them their bed and slowly introduce them to the rest of the house. You need to housebreak your puppy, too, so familiarize them with the area where you will train them for this.

- Finally, keep handy equipment ready. This includes enough toys, food and water bowls, leads, collars, name tags, puppy grooming tools, car safety equipment, and anything else you need.

I found that I learned a lot about this process as I went along. I had to change collars, found that one type of food did not suit my puppy, and found that she got car sick frequently. So whenever I saw something going wrong, I adjusted and adapted, and we got through it fine. The main thing is to keep your hopes high and let this be a learning experience for both you and your little puppy.

2

SIMPLE STEP-BY-STEP TRAINING FOR KIDS

Are you ready to begin training your puppy? Puppy training will help your little friend socialize with other pets and humans. It includes good behavior and obedience. Ideally, you should take 15 minutes to train your puppy every day. This can be in short bursts of activity (say 5 minutes spread three times throughout the day). If you find your puppy is becoming tired and losing focus, give them a break, or continue the session a few hours later. Be flexible because this is a learning experience for both of you.

TEACHING YOUR PUPPY IT'S OKAY TO BE ALONE

Puppies are social creatures. They do amazingly well in the presence of people they love. This being said, they need to learn to be comfortable with themselves. So, training them to be alone is essential. Begin by teaching them to stay confined in a safe zone like their crate. Follow these steps to help train your puppy to become confident of staying alone.

- Associate the crate as a comfortable space for your puppy. Give them treats in it, play with them, and praise them when they sit quietly in the crate.

- A time will come when they will enter the crate on their own because *it will feel like their safe place, a little personal hide-out.* This means you can begin training them to stay alone.

- Train them by leaving them alone in the confinement area with a toy. Come back immediately and praise them for being a good puppy. Slowly increase the amount of time you leave them alone, beginning from 1 minute to 2 hours.

- After three-four months of training, you can start leaving them alone for little time intervals. Never let it be more than four hours at the start.

- It is important to remember that your puppy has never been alone before. Be gentle with them, and don't worry if you come back to find your house is a mess. Give them plenty of time to adjust to a new routine.

WHEN TO START TRAINING YOUR PUPPY

Your puppy's training will begin as soon as they come home. Your puppy will learn things from their environment and process these things in their own time. Don't worry about waiting too long before training them, because you will find that they begin to catch on from their early days.

Basic commands like "sit," "down," and "stay" can be taught as early as seven to eight weeks.

Use methods based on *positive reinforcement* and be gentle if you begin training your puppy at seven to eight weeks of age. They have shorter attention spans, so start with brief, daily sessions (Horwitz, 2021).

TEACHiNG YOuR PuPPY THEiR NAME

I'm excited to tell you that your puppy will learn their name naturally based on how you address them and how often you use their name. But, it is better to encourage this process with a few tricks.

Step 1:

Begin by trying to engage your puppy's attention. Do this when it is just your puppy and you at home with no distractions. Don't start if your puppy is over-excited, exhausted, or too distracted by something. Keep a bag of treats to help the process.

Step 2:

Say your puppy's name once, in a warm, loving, happy voice. If this doesn't get their attention (they don't know their name yet), stop for a minute. Then, try again and add a sharp clap or a kissing noise. Make sure you look happy and smiling.

Step 3:

As soon as your puppy responds by giving you their attention, reward by saying, *"Good!"* or "That's *a good girl/boy!"* Click if you are using a clicker. This is called *Marking*. Then, give your puppy a treat. This will be the puppy's initial connection to responding to their name. Follow the below points in order to master the training.

- Now, let your puppy get distracted again. After a minute, repeat the whole process. Make sure to mark and reward every time your puppy responds by giving you their attention.

- Repeat this eight to ten times in one sitting, but no more. Too much, and your puppy will get bored and wonder what the fuss is about.

- Please repeat the above steps three to four times every day. Your puppy will soon learn that they will be rewarded and praised whenever you call their name if they respond with their attention.

- Puppies have very low attention spans. So, change it up. Take them to different locations of your house and your backyard. It can be anywhere quiet and with no distractions. Repeat the steps we talked about. Your puppy will gradually begin responding to their name no matter where you take them.

- After one to two weeks of training, Slowly begin increasing the time intervals for giving the treat. So, call out their name, mark when they respond with *"Good!"* but pause for two seconds before giving them the treat. This means they have to hold their attention for two seconds longer.

- Increase the two seconds to three, then four, and eventually, take it to a place where your puppy can wait ten seconds without a treat.

- If your puppy has trouble concentrating, immediately return to the first stage of giving them the treat at the two-second interval. This means that you have increased the time too soon and your puppy is feeling overwhelmed.

- Remember, we want our puppies to be engaged. If we try too much too soon, we will lose their interest. So, stay flexible.

- Once you have a full ten seconds of your puppy's attention, it's time to amp up the games. Start introducing toys to distract them. Begin by doing this in one room.

- When they are distracted with the toy, call out their name.

- If they respond, immediately mark it and treat them. You don't need to pause before treating at this stage because your puppy is giving you attention over something they like.

- You can keep them on a leash which will help them through this process.

- If your puppy starts to move away or get too distracted, gently put them back in their position by tugging at the leash.

- Just like how you are raising the difficulty level, also increase the treats. Introduce something they will love- like chicken liver, bacon treats, or beef jerky (anything friendly for puppies).

- Once your puppy can turn to you and pay attention even when distracted, begin increasing the attention time from two seconds to ten seconds.

- Now, change up the locations again. Practice with the toy or any other distraction in different rooms. Try the backyard, wherever you wish to, as long as your full attention is on your puppy. When you begin at a new location, start by immediately rewarding them if they respond to your call. Gradually increase the attention time. Since they are moving and learning in different environments, they need some time to adjust.

- You're almost there, but don't stop yet. The home run happens with regular repetition. Remember, *practice makes perfect!* Go through the exercise a few times in the day, in different environments. Try different distractions so that your puppy has to work at giving you their attention.

- Incorporate the exercise into walks when you take your puppy out to a pet store or a park, in other people's houses, everywhere- the idea is to reach a stage where you have your puppy's attention no matter how interesting the distractions are.

- When your puppy fully learns to respond to their name, it becomes easier to teach them other commands. They already associate their name with something positive and rewarding.

- So, say you want to keep them out of trouble, you can just do it by calling out their name, and they will turn to you- *because they associate that with praise and treats!*

After a few weeks practicing, you should be in a good place with this exercise. Remember to keep it fun and flexible, and don't push too hard if you see your puppy is getting tired. Here are some important things to make this simpler for your fur friend and you:

- Never call their name angrily. Always be happy, gentle, and positive.

- Don't call their name for any tasks they won't like, such as trimming nails or going to the vet. Of course, you need their attention for that, so call and distract them as if you were calling for some other purpose. Wait till some time has passed, then trim their nails or take them to the vet. *Your puppy should never associate their name with an unpleasant experience.*

- When you begin teaching commands, don't use their name with the command if you already have their attention.

- If you don't have their attention, call their name, pause for a second, then give the command. This ensures they don't confuse different training activities.

- Finally, have lots of fun in the process. It's a great opportunity to find the little quirks that make your pup special, so enjoy every second.

BASIC TRAINING COMMANDS

When you begin training, start with the simple things. The most straightforward commands are *'sit,' 'lie,'* and *'stay.'* We will discuss these in detail in Chapter 3, but let me give you a simple breakdown here.

TRAINING YOUR PUPPY TO SIT

Teaching your puppy to sit is a very good way to ease them into training.

Step 1:

When your puppy is in a standing position, hold a treat in front of them.

Step 2:

Keep the treat close to your puppy's nose.

Step 3:

Now, slowly circle the treat like an arc over your puppy's head.

Step 4:

Your puppy will raise their heady to copy your hand's motion of moving the treat.

Step 5:

As they raise their head, their bottom will go on the floor.

Step 6:

As soon as they sit, mark with praise and give them the treat.

- Repeat this process five to six times, spread throughout the day. Don't make each session longer than five minutes.
- After a few days, as soon as your puppy sits down, add the cue word *"sit."* Be careful not to say it before they sit down. Keep your tone loving and happy.
- Practice this five to six times a day, and reward them when they sit.

Your puppy will eventually learn to associate the cue word and the treat as rewards for sitting. Remember to keep the sessions fun for both of you. Use a lot of praise to keep your puppy's morale up.

TRAINING YOUR PUPPY TO LIE

Step 1:

Keep your puppy's favorite treat in your hand.

Step 2:

Ask your puppy to sit, ensuring that they have seen the treat in your hand.

Step 3:

Slowly move your hand down to the ground in front of their feet.

Step 4:

Wait till your puppy imitates your hand motion and lies down.

Step 5:

Praise and reward immediately.

- After practicing this five to six times, spread over five-minute sessions for a few days, add the cue word *"Down/ Lie."* Add this cue when they lie down, not before.
- Practice until your puppy associates lying down with the verbal cue and a treat.

This is slightly more complicated than teaching your puppy to sit, so don't be disheartened or give up too soon. Keep trying, and your puppy will learn to lie down in no time.

TEACHING YOUR PUPPY TO STAY

Step 1:

Your puppy needs to be comfortable with the *lie/down* command before you begin teaching this command.

Step 2:

Begin by asking your puppy to lie down.

Step 3:

Give your puppy a hand signal. It can be a simple *stop* signal with the palm of your hand facing your puppy.

Step 4:

Don't give a treat immediately.

Step 5:

After a few seconds, say *"stay"* and reward your puppy with a treat. Do this only if they are still lying down and have not gotten up.

Step 6:

If they got up, repeat the process without a treat. If you see your puppy getting frustrated, stop for a few minutes, and begin again.

- Practice this five to six times spread throughout the day. Don't keep sessions longer than ten minutes.
- Once your puppy learns the basic *stay* command, amp up the difficulty by increasing the physical distance between you and them. If they still stay in the lying position and wait for you to come, give them the treat, reward them immediately.
- Practice in different locations so that there's a change of space.

Teaching your puppy to stay with a command will help you keep them safe. Say you are taking your puppy out from the car and attach a lead to their collar. If they know the *stay* command, they won't be over-excited. It's a discipline mechanism that will teach your puppy to obey you.

HOUSE AND POTTY TRAINING FOR YOUR PUPPY

Training your puppy good house and potty behaviors will ensure that your home environment is clean and friendly. *Make sure to take the advice and help of your guardians for these activities.* They require patience and guidance, so the more hands-on-deck, the better. It can take up to four to six months before your puppy is fully housebroken. Some puppies may take longer, so don't be disheartened, and don't set a rigid timeline.

The size of your puppy can influence how many times they have to go. Smaller breeds have smaller bladders, plus a higher metabolism, which culminates in more trips outdoors. Don't worry about setbacks because accidents will happen. They happened to us when we were kids too. Just try to take your puppy out at the first sign that they need to do their business and reward them for reinforcing good habits.

You can start house and potty training when your puppy is between 12 to 16 weeks old. By then, they have sufficient bladder and bowel control and will learn to hold it till the location is right. These points will help you get started.

- Begin by keeping your puppy in a designated space. This may be a crate, a room, or on their lead. As the puppy learns that they need to go outside, increase their freedom to roam the house.

- Keep your puppy on a timely feeding schedule. Don't give them food (except treats while training) between meals.

- Look for signs to understand when your puppy needs to go. They all have typical signs like going around the same spot in circles, sniffing the floor, looking restless, or repeatedly going to a room where they may have done their business before.

- Take your puppy out first thing after they wake up in order to do their business. Accept help from your guardians for this step.

- Repeat this step once every 30 minutes to an hour.

- Also, do this after they finish every meal or after they wake up from a nap.

- Make sure they go out once before sleeping at night.

- Night training will take time. You must remember your puppy is small and still learning bladder control, so don't be surprised if you wake up to a mess. To lessen this, keep a pee-pad or paper away from their bed so that they have the opportunity to relieve themselves if it is urgent.

- Take your puppy to eliminate at the same spot every time. They will associate a scent with the location, which will encourage them to go.

- Stay by their side.

- When your puppy does their business outside at the designated spot, praise and give them a treat. You can also take them for a short walk around the neighborhood, but make sure you bring a bag for them in case you need it.

- During the first few months, it's better not to leave your puppy alone. It would help if you did that after they are already housebroken. If it is an emergency, spend some time exercising and trying to get your puppy to go before you leave the house. Leave a paper/absorbent pee-pad in a location they are comfortable with, away from the living room and your sleeping area. This is just in case an accident happens; you don't want to create a habit with it.

The best way to ensure your puppy learns good housebreaking habits is to be consistent. Keep at it, forgive their mistakes, reward them when they go to the right place at the right time, and you will get there.

FOOD LuRE TRAiNiNG

By now, you are aware that puppies respond positively when we encourage them with treats. This is called *Luring*, and it's positive reinforcement for your puppy. They associate a specific behavior as something they must do to get a treat from you, and it becomes a joyful activity for them. Follow these points to master the food lure training.

- Small pieces of food or puppy treats are used to motivate your puppy to learn good behavior. These are rewards.

- If the rewards are tasty, the puppy gives the desired response when you show it to them because they know that this will get them the treat.

- For example, if you hold a treat over your puppy's nose and make an arc, you will be able to teach them to sit. If you place it on the ground in front of their feet, they will learn to lie. In the same way, most commands can be taught with positive reinforcements. Gradually, you should pair a cue word with every action and then give the treat for the appropriate response. This will help your puppy learn the meaning of each command.

- So, the treat becomes a tool to get your puppy into different positions. Once your puppy has obeyed your command, pat and adore them, and give sufficient verbal praise. These become your secondary reinforcers.

- You have to phase out the lure and treat rewards gradually. You cannot keep giving them food every time they obey you because that will cause an unhealthy attachment with food.

- As your puppy begins to obey your commands more quickly, start by hiding the food and giving only the verbal command. Increase the number of times they have to perform a task to get a treat. But keep your verbal praise intact.

- For example, ask them to sit five times before giving them one treat. But, every time they sit, reward with praise and pats.

- In time, your puppy will learn to respond to your verbal cues and hand gestures without needing treats.

The positive verbal cues and pats will become stronger reinforcements since they have been paired with treats in the past. Your puppy will associate these as rewards for good behavior and please you to get your attention and love.

A PUPPY TRAINING SCHEDULE BASED ON THEIR AGE

Here's a simple truth. While puppies are a delight, there will be moments of exasperation and frustration. The important part is to remain consistent in your efforts to train your puppy, establish a daily routine, and respond to them. It becomes more difficult if you are unresponsive- it's like you coming home with an A on a test and getting no response from your family.

A puppy's time to learn basic things will depend on many factors, one of them being age. Here are some tips you can follow, based on your puppy's age.

- At all stages, teach your puppy to be comfortable in their crate. The crate should be their environment, full of things they love.

- If you start training a seven-week-old puppy, begin with the simple stuff. Teach them to identify their food and water bowls, what time of the day they will eat, what time they will sleep, when they will go out to do their business, and what spot in the house is their grooming area. At this stage, you are familiarizing your puppy with their home. You can also teach them the basics of good behavior- like associating something they must not do with vigorously shaking your head and saying "No!"

- If you are training an eight-week-old puppy, go through all the previous stages. Additionally, begin teaching them to be calm indoors. Teach them not to nip at anyone's feet or grab things. Reward if they are gentle while taking something from your hand instead of grabbing it. Teach your puppy not to be jumpy or excitable and open their mouth if they hold something they shouldn't. At all stages, your puppy must consider you as the pack leader.

- If your puppy is ten weeks old, follow all the previous steps. Once they are comfortable, begin training them to walk on a lead without pulling. Teach them to wait at open gates till you call for them to come in. Teach them to respond when you call their name. Also, begin teaching them to be quiet in the house. This will take patience, especially with some vocal breeds like corgis and huskies. But enough good reinforcement will get you there.

- Training your puppy when they are 12 weeks should begin with all the previous steps. Additionally, teach them the *sit* command. Teach them other obedience traits like going to bed when they are told. This will help them learn impulse control and make them calmer.

- If you train your puppy at 16 weeks, go through the previous steps. Also, begin taking them for structured walks where they stay by your side and pay attention to you. Teach them to greet passers-by and other dogs by being friendly and calm or not greet them at all. They should not jump and act over-excited whenever they see someone new.

By six months, your puppy should have picked up all these habits. Don't worry if you begin your training a little late because what matters is how systematic and consistent you are.

CRATE TRAINING YOUR PUPPY

The crate is like a second home for your puppy. Never associate anything negative with it. Instead, it is a space your puppy retires to when they are sleepy or tired. It's their den, much like your personal bedroom or nursery. So, choose a good crate. The size should fit your puppy and leave room for them to walk around in it. There should be enough floor space for bedding, a water bowl, and a mat. Metal crates work the best because of their collapsible nature. Be careful with fabric ones because your puppy can chew through them. Follow these steps for easy training.

- Once you have a crate, set it up in a quiet space in your room, a spot where your puppy will come to relax or simply spend time on their own.

- You may find that your puppy is curious about the crate and will begin investigating it as soon you set it up. Make sure to keep the crate door secured open so that it won't shut on them, which will scare and negatively impact them. Reward your dog if you see positive signs of curiosity in getting to know the crate. This can be with treats, praise, anything that works.

- Not all puppies will begin exploring right away. Some may even be a bit wary and afraid of the crate at first. Don't worry if this happens. Put your puppy's favorite toy and some treats near the crate. As they gain confidence, they will go near it. Reward this with praise. Next, put the toys and treats inside the crate, and leave the door open. Your puppy will slowly begin going in to eat the treats and play. Reward their behavior. With time, they will begin moving in and out of the crate freely.

- Your puppy will begin spending time in the crate without any worries. At this stage, begin feeding them their meals in the crate. This will help them associate being in the crate with a positive experience. Add a verbal cue when you are serving their food, like *"crate,"* so they know that they have to go in it to get their meal. They may begin to go to their crate automatically during meal times.

- When your puppy is settling in happily with the crate door open, begin closing it. Close the door after your puppy starts eating, and open it before they finish their meal. This will help them understand that the closed-door is ordinary, nothing to be scared of. If they get anxious, begin by closing half the door first and then fully once they are more comfortable.

- Gradually increase the period for which the door is closed. If they become anxious, open it immediately, and then try again at the next mealtime.

- After a few times of practicing this, step one foot away for a minute and then come back. If your puppy gets excited or stressed, stand away from the crate, stay calm, and give them a verbal cue like *"stay."* Return to them once they have calmed down.

- Once your puppy becomes more comfortable with you moving around, you can step away from the crate or outside the room for a few seconds while they have their meal. Return if you hear them barking, and try again during the next meal.

- After your puppy becomes comfortable with all these steps, begin training them to be in the crate outside their mealtimes. Your puppy should be comfortable with the verbal cue *"crate"* by now, and you can use it to send them in and reward them for doing it. Once they are comfortable being in the crate without food, close the door gently for a few seconds.

- Practice this a few times, and then increase the period for which the door is closed.

- As they become comfortable, you can begin training them to treat the crate as their personal space by stepping away from it, a little at a time.

With crate training, the secret lies in consistent positive reinforcement. Make sure your puppy's crate appeals to them. While you can keep them in the crate after they are trained, I would recommend not leaving them alone for more than three to four hours at a time. Make sure they have regular access to it, and not just when you are going out. Also, to avoid any accidents, make sure your puppy has done their business before tucking them in the crate for a nap or because you have to step away for some time.

SOCiALiZiNG YOUR PUPPY

Socializing your puppy will help them to be confident and self-assured. They will respond to their environment with positive curiosity without becoming nervous, over-excited, or fearful. Socializing will equip your puppy with the necessary life skills to make friends and be chirpy and happy. We all want friends to be around us in good and bad times, and it's no different for puppies. Here are few points to consider to help socialize your puppy.

- Just like us, puppies are not born with a dictionary of how to behave in social situations. We learn these things from our families. In the same way, puppies learn how to behave from how their owners guide and train them.

- A socialized puppy can have pleasant interactions with other puppies and dogs and with adult humans, children, vets, and other animals. They also become sensitive to environmental cues, like traffic signals, crowds, traveling in a car, and other sights and sounds.

- Socialized puppies are naturally open and prone to exploring everything. They begin learning what constitutes their home: your family and you and the outside world.

- Up until 16 weeks of age, this primary socialization will help your puppy understand their territory and behave with different social groups. Experience is everything, and the more you encourage your puppy to explore, the better they will become calm and well-behaved in all situations.

- At all points, if you see your puppy doing something they shouldn't, don't respond harshly. They may not even know why it is wrong. Instead, interrupt and distract them with a toy, and then reward them when they do what you ask them to.

- Discourage activities like constant barking, jumping, nipping, chewing, or mounting. These may seem cute when they are puppies but will make them antisocial later. Always be gentle when discouraging. Say *"no,"* then distract them. They will eventually associate the word *no* with something they should not do.

Finally, never hesitate to ask for help during the socialization process. The more you involve other family members, the more people your puppy becomes comfortable around. This ensures that they obey commands from your family with ease. It will also make them comfortable in more extensive social situations when you won't be the only one around.

TRAINING YOUR PUPPY LOOSE-LEASH WALKING

Teaching your puppy to walk confidently on a leash, is a way for both of you to enjoy your walks. Let's face it; no one would want to walk a puppy who is constantly pulling on the leash and making them run. It would be so uncomfortable.

- The first step is to make sure your puppy feels comfortable on the leash. They may snap and bite at the leash initially-because it's natural to feel uncomfortable when something is around your neck. So, treat your puppy every time they put the leash on without complaint. Try to get them to stay still with the *sit* command. That will make it easier for you.

- Next, stand beside your puppy and wait till they are standing quietly without fussing. Hold the leash in a loose loop. Once they stand quietly, reward them with praise and a treat.

- Take one step, and ask your puppy to follow you. Give them a treat when they catch up.

- Start walking slowly. Don't pull the leash at any time. Give verbal encouragement so that your puppy stays in tune with you, and reward them with treats when they keep even pace.

- If they run in front, turn in the opposite direction, call them back to you, and reward them for coming back. Continue walking as before.

- Gradually increase the period between giving treats.

- Allow your puppy to explore their surroundings when they are walking. Pause and let them smell the road, the flowers, the bushes, whatever strikes their fancy. After some time, call out to them in a happy voice and praise them when they begin walking again.

Eventually, your puppy will walk happily at your side when they are on the leash. A well-trained puppy is a joy to watch when they walk down the street. And you will be so proud when their good behavior is noticed. Be patient with leash training, and take a guardian/helper with you at the initial stages.

TEACHiNG YOUR PUPPY TO COME WHEN CALLED

We are almost at the end of Chapter 2! Before we move on, I'll say a few words to help you train your puppy to come when you call them. This is handy for crowded rooms, when you want your puppy near you, or when you are trying to get them away from any troublesome situation.

- Sit with your puppy and say the verbal cue, *'come.'*

- Each time you repeat the verbal cue, give them a treat. They don't have to do anything at this stage. Just repeat the word and treat them.

- Then, drop a treat on the floor nearby. Once your puppy comes and eats the treat, repeat the verbal cue. Reward them when they look up.

- Repeat this step a few times. Then, toss the treat a little further so that they go the distance to get it. Then, move closer to your puppy and give the verbal cue. When they turn around to face you, show the treat in your hand and repeat the cue. When they come to you, give them the treat.

- Add movement little by little, and make the process more interesting. Toss a treat to your puppy; take a few steps away while calling the verbal cue. Wait for them to come running to you after finishing the treat.

- When they catch you, reward them with praise and another treat. It should be like a game for them, where they get rewards for catching you.

When your puppy reaches you, don't grab at them. This may confuse or frighten them. Instead, give a gentle laugh and present them with a treat. This reinforces their attachment to you and makes everything more fun for them.

KEY POINTS

Whew! Look at how many new things you learned! I'm sure you cannot wait to begin trying these on your puppy. Here are some key points to help you further.

- Don't leave your puppy alone in the house for more than two to four hours. Especially if they are in the training phase, try not to leave them alone at all.

- Associate the crate as a positive space where your puppy will go to rest and relax. Don't attach any negative emotions to the crate.

- Consistency and patience are key tools that will help you train your puppy.

- Use positive reinforcements like treats and encouraging words. Never scold your puppy for mistakes.

- Begin socializing your puppy from their early age so that they become confident and self-assured around other animals and people.

- While leash-training, be gentle and patient. Don't pull on the leash.

- Don't let training sessions be too long, because your puppy will get bored and confused.

- Train your puppy in different rooms of the house and the backyard. This will give them variety and make things more fun.

- Be patient with housebreaking your puppy, and let your guardians guide you through this process. Make sure to take them out once when they wake up, and once before bedtime.

Finally, enjoy yourself! This training phase will not return, and you will soon come to cherish it as the start of beautiful memories of bonding with your furry friend. Don't be hard on your puppy, and don't be hard on yourself either. Learn as you go, and your puppy will grow into a happy, beautiful dog.

3

SIMPLE
TRAINING
COMMANDS

You must teach your puppy good behavior and discipline. This will not only make you proud but also raise your puppy's confidence and social acceptance. Unruly, undisciplined puppies can be challenging to be around.

The good news is that, with regular sessions, your puppy will be well-behaved in no time. Before we begin, here are some things for you to remember.

- Be patient with your puppy. Have training sessions regularly.
- Don't push too hard when you start.
- Make sure your training locations are quiet and without distractions.
- Keep your lessons short, sweet, and simple.
- Never punish your puppy for a mistake. Rather, gently distract them and try again after a short break.
- Reward liberally.
- Teach your puppy a new command after they learn the old ones.
- Train your puppy as if you are playing games with them.

- Be a friend to your puppy. This is a great way to make it fun and exciting for both of you (*15 Essential Commands to Teach Your Dog*, 2016).

Most of the commands they need to learn are simple. Let's go through them one-by-one.

THE "SIT" COMMAND

We read about the *"Sit"* command briefly in the last chapter. It's a neat way to teach your puppy to be obedient. Plus, it's a simple command, and your puppy will learn it in no time.

Step 1:

Start by first holding a treat in your hand, just visible enough to your puppy.

Step 2:

Gently move the treat around your puppy's head in an arc.

Step 3:

Your puppy will follow the motion and eventually sit down.

Step 4:

As soon as they sit down, say *"sit"* clearly, and give them the treat.

Step 5:

Repeat four to five times until they associate the verbal cue and getting the treat with sitting down.

Step 6:

After four to five days, begin phasing out the treat.

Step 7:

Keep the treat in your hand, but don't give it to your puppy. Instead, say *"sit."* Praise heartily when they sit down.

Step 8:

Wait for them to stand up without giving them the treat.

Step 9:

Repeat two to three times in the beginning, then provide them with the treat. Gradually increase the intervals.

Eventually, your puppy will associate sitting down as a way to earn your praise and do it without the treat.

THE "LiE DOWN" COMMAND

"Down" is a simple command, and your puppy will learn it easily if you train them uniformly.

Don't confuse your puppy by using the same verbal cue for different actions. For example, if you want them to get down from the bed, don't use the *"down"* command. Instead, use another cue like *"get off!"*

Set aside ten-minute sessions to train your puppy. Repeat these sessions five to six times a day. Don't overexert them. You don't want them to look at training as a punishment or something boring. Rather, make it interesting.

Be happy and friendly when you are training them.

Step 1:

Begin by holding a treat in your hand with a bit part exposed so that your puppy can just see it.

Step 2:

Show the treat to your puppy, and make sure you have their undivided attention.

Step 3:

Place your hand flat on the floor with the treat under it.

Step 4:

Your puppy will begin to look for ways to retrieve it.

Step 5:

Eventually, they will lie down. The moment they do, praise them verbally or using the clicker, and give them the treat.

Step 6:

Add the verbal cue *"down."*

Step 7:

Repeat this process till they learn that your hand on the floor means they have to lie down.

After a few days, increase the time interval for giving treats. Put your hand down, make them lie, say the verbal cue *"down,"* but then stand up again without giving them the treat. Repeat this once more. If they lie down the second time, praise and give the treat.

With time, your puppy will associate your hand coming down and the verbal cue *"down"* as an instruction for them to lie. Since you praise them whenever they do it, they will do it simply to get your love. Puppies are very loving animals. They will do anything for the affection of their humans. So, be unfailing in your efforts, and you will succeed.

THE "COME" COMMAND

"Come" is an important command you will teach your puppy. It will help you to keep them out of trouble. Anytime you see them heading for a potentially dangerous situation, you can call out the command, and they will return to you. For this, you must train them to respond to the command.

The key to success with this command is beginning early (within six to eight weeks). Young puppies *love* following their humans around. After six months, your puppy will become more independent.

Ask a guardian to help you teach this command.

Step 1:

Get your guardian to kneel on the floor.

Step 2:

Keep your puppy seated close to your guardian.

Step 3:

Stand in front of your pet with a treat in your hand.

Step 4:

Call them to you with the verbal cue *"come"!* And also move your arm towards you while moving a step back.

Step 5:

They will hear the excitement and happiness in your voice and come to you.

Step 6:

Greet them with open arms and lots of praise and give them the treat.

Step 7:

Repeat this a few times.

Step 8:

Next, once they are used to this, sit a few paces away.

Step 9:

Call them again, showing them the treat in your hand.

Step 10:

As soon as they come to you, give them the treat and lavish them with praise.

Practice for five-ten minutes, spread out five to six times in a day. Change the locations to keep things interesting. Keep increasing the distance between your puppy and you every few minutes. Follow the below points to master the training.

- Once they have learned the command, amp it up. Start playing hide and seek by hiding in different corners of your home and asking them to come.

- Move this to your backyard.

- Make it difficult by adding some distractions like their favorite toy, asking a friend to distract them, and asking them to come from a distance.

- Once your puppy has learned to move beyond distractions and still come to you when you give the verbal cue, take them out with an extendable leash or long training line, which will provide them with some freedom.

- Practice this in the park or a safe space, not a busy road.

- Let them outpace you, and then ask them to come with the verbal cue. Keep a treat and reward them when they come back to you.

- Don't worry if this last step takes some time, because there will be so many exciting distractions. Squirrels, hedges, other dogs- your puppy is bound to be distracted.

- Instead, if you find they are not coming back, go up to them, be affectionate and gentle, reduce the distance between the two of you, and try again.

Your puppy has to associate coming to you with an action that will be rewarding for them. Remember that they don't need to come to you. They are doing it to please you and gain your approval. So, be kind, happy, and loving. You'll succeed.

THE "NO" COMMAND

The *"No"* command is a great way to make sure your puppy stays out of trouble. Puppies are curious little creatures, getting their noses into everything. They sense things by smell and feel, so don't be surprised if you find them sniffing everywhere. But, if they know the *"no"* command, you'll be able to keep them safe from sniffing anything dangerous.

Step 1:

Get a set of dog-training discs. These are little metal discs joined on a key fob. You can hold them without making any noise. At the exact moment, you say *"no,"* drop to make a sound that your puppy won't hear anywhere else.

Step 2:

Keep some treats ready. This training technique will work in two ways. Whenever your puppy obeys you, they get a treat. When they don't, you drop the disc. If you drop the disc, don't give them a treat. This reinforces that they did something wrong.

Step 3:

Begin by placing a treat on the floor away from your puppy.

Step 4:

When your puppy goes to eat the treat, gently move the discs in your hand and say *"no."* Don't rattle them too loudly, or else your puppy will become frightened. Say *"no"* loud and clear- they should hear it.

Step 5:

Remove the treat quickly, without letting them eat it.

Step 6:

Repeat this till your puppy begins to associate the sound of the discs with not getting a treat. Eventually, they will be disappointed and give up.

Step 7:

Now, ask them to perform another action, like *"sit."* When they obey, immediately reward them with verbal praise and a treat.

- Repeat the whole process.
- Your puppy will come to associate both the disc and the verbal cue *"no"* to imply they should not do something.
- After three to four days of practicing with the discs, remove them and only practice with the verbal cue.
- With time, your puppy will understand that they must not do something when you say *"no."* If they do, you will be unhappy and won't reward them. Be patient, and if you find that the discs are making your puppy anxious, try an alternative like a little bell or a whistle. Don't use something that will drown out your voice because your puppy must hear your verbal cue.

THE "LEAVE IT" COMMAND

Like the *"no"* command, *"leave it"* will help you establish control over your puppy, especially if they are naughty. Say you are out on a walk, and your puppy sees an exciting rock on the road. They proceed to eat it. If they know the *"leave it"* command, you can say it, and they will leave the rock alone, allowing you to continue your walk in peace.

Both *"no"* and *"leave it"* are restrictive commands meant to protect your puppy from self-harm.

You can use the discs to train them for this command as well.

Step 1:

Put a tasty treat within your puppy's reach.

Step 2:

When they go to take the treat, say *"leave it"* and rattle the disc. Make sure they can hear your voice over the disc.

Step 3:

Wait ten seconds and see if they try to take the treat. If they try, rattle and repeat the verbal cue.

Step 4:

If they don't take the treat, which you are asking them to leave (the training treat), reward them with another treat (don't give them the one with which you are training them).

- Keep practicing, gradually increasing the time interval for which your puppy has to wait to get a treat.

- Don't be harsh if they fail a few times. Pause, and try again.

- After four to five days of practicing with the discs and verbal commands, stop using them and use only your verbal command.

Like with the previous command, your puppy will understand that when you say *"leave it,"* they must not take something. The advantages of teaching this go above just protecting them. Say you drop something on the floor with lots of traffic, and your puppy runs to it immediately. Maybe it's an important piece of paper. If they know this command, you will save it from puppy destruction.

THE "STAY" COMMAND

The *"stay"* command is relatively simple and will help keep your puppy disciplined. You love your puppy's boisterous cuteness, but some people may get overwhelmed by it. If the puppy knows this command, they will be toned down in front of other animals and strangers.

Step 1:

Ask your puppy to sit down.

Step 2:

Slowly back away.

Step 3:

If they come toward you, say *"no"* clearly.

Step 4:

If they stop in their tracks, say the verbal cue *"stay,"* reward with a treat, and praise.

Step 5:

Now, try to increase the distance between you and your puppy after four to five intervals.

- Repeat this a few times, and increase the time intervals for giving treats.

- Take it outside. Walk your puppy on a loose lead, let them go ahead of you, and say, *"stay."* Reward them each time they stop for the first four to five times, gradually increasing time intervals. Praise them throughout, and keep your face happy and loving.

Your puppy will understand that if you say *"stay,"* you ask them to halt and wait. They will obey your verbal cue without the need for a treat.

THE "GET OFF" COMMAND

Teaching your puppy the *"get off"* command will help you get your spot on the couch/bed when they are hogging it. It's kinder to give them a verbal cue rather than picking them up and putting them down. That may also make them feel unwanted. So, here's what you have to do. Also, some puppies are pro-counter-surfers. They can jump up on counters to steal food, so knowing this command helps.

Step 1:

When your puppy puts their paws or body up on something, like a sofa or a counter, say the verbal cue *"get off"* and lure them down with a treat.

Step 2:

Don't give them the treat until they come down.

Step 4:

As soon as they come down, praise and give the treat.

Step 5:

Repeat this as many times as they climb up on a surface. This step is important. *Do not force them to get up to train this command. They will get confused.* Instead, wait for the next time they climb up and repeat the steps.

After four to five days of training with the treat, increase the time interval. For instance, treat only once every four times they climb up. Instead, use the verbal cue with a smiling, happy face. Whenever they come down, praise lavishly.

Your puppy will soon realize that whenever you say *"get off,"* they must come down. If they don't, you will be disappointed. If they do, you will praise and adore them. This positive reinforcement will make them come down.

THE "WATCH ME" COMMAND

"Watch Me" is a lesser-known but handy command. It is very useful when you bring your puppy to a busy area, say a crowded street or a walking lane with too many birds or squirrels. This command will help them stay focused on you.

Step 1:

Hold a treat near your puppy's face.

Step 2:

Begin moving the treat towards your face until it is just in front of your nose.

Step 3:

Wait till they establish eye contact with you.

Step 4:

As soon as they do, add the verbal cue *"Watch me,"* reward with the treat, and praise.

Step 5:

Repeat four to five times, gradually increasing the time interval of giving treats.

After a few tries, your puppy will know that when you say *"watch me,"* they must look at you. If they do, they will get love and praise. Use this command whenever you need to keep their attention on you.

THE "WAIT" COMMAND

The *"Wait"* command is an essential one. It will help you teach appropriate social conduct to your puppy. For example, say you have guests coming. The moment you open the door, your puppy charges at them. This will surprise them and may even scare some. To prevent this, train them with the *"wait"* command.

Step 1:

Take the help of a guardian when training your puppy to wait.

Step 2:

Go to the door of your apartment or house with your puppy.

Step 3:

Stand inside, just facing the door, keeping your puppy beside you. Use a loose lead to keep them in position so that they don't wander off.

Step 4:

Have a guardian stand outside.

Step 5:

Ask your guardian to open the door.

Step 6:

If your puppy lunges as soon as the door is open, ask your guardian to shut it immediately, and you add the verbal cue *"wait."*

Step 7:

Repeat this till your puppy becomes disappointed and cools down.

Eventually, your puppy will wait. If they wait, then reward them with a treat and praise them.

This trick takes some time because puppies are wired to be over-loving. They see people, and they have to show them their affection, so learning this is not intrinsic to their nature. Be regular with this, and make sure your guardian closes the door every time you say "*wait.*" This will tell them that they won't get to greet your guardian if they don't wait. They will get the hang of it with time.

THE "DROP IT" COMMAND

"Drop it" is an excellent command to keep your puppies from harming themselves and destroying valuables in your house. To teach them this command, you'll need two identical toys.

Step 1:

Give one of the two toys to your puppy.

Step 2:

Say the verbal cue *"drop it"* and show them the other toy.

Step 3:

When they drop the first toy, reward and praise them.

Step 4:

Repeat this four to five times. Add the verbal cue whenever you show them the second toy, which symbolizes an object to which you want to draw their attention.

Step 5:

Praise each time they drop the toy they are holding in their mouth, and give them the other toy.

After a few takes, your puppy will begin to realize that *"drop it"* means they must let go of whatever they are holding in your mouth. Keeping a toy in your hand helps. For example, say your puppy picks up a shoe from the rack. You can immediately show them a toy and say, *"drop it."* This will tell them that if they drop the shoe, they will get the toy, plus lots of praise, and even a treat sometimes.

THE "HANDLE YOUR BUSINESS" COMMAND

Housebreaking your puppy will take time and patience. Remember one key thing- teach them this command in *one location* where you want them to go. Don't change locations because this will confuse and disorient them. The spot you choose will mean that they go there to do their business regularly. We've talked about housebreaking your puppy in sufficient detail in the last chapter, so I'll just highlight what you need to remember.

Step 1:

Use one command, like *"Go Potty."*

Step 2:

Take them out once every morning as soon as they wake up and once before they go to sleep at night.

Step 3:

Look out for signs like them scratching the floor, going around in circles, or looking restless.

Step 4:

Once they do their business in the chosen spot, praise lavishly. Tell them how good they are and reward them.

Step 5:

Take them to the same spot daily. Eventually, they will associate the smell of the place with having to go. This will become a habit.

Be patient when training this command. After all, your puppy is very small and has a small bladder too. Keep pads around for accidents, and never scold or punish them. If they have an accident, just take them to their designated spot and repeat the verbal cue. This will remind them where they have to go.

THE "TAKE IT" COMMAND

This is a lesser-known trick, but it's a great way to bond and have fun with your pup. Whenever you want your puppy to pick something up, you can use this trick.

Step 1:

Hold your puppy's favorite toy in front of their face.

Step 2:

When they reach out to take it, add the verbal cue *"take it."*

Step 3:

Reward and praise when they take the toy.

Your puppy will soon associate the verbal command as a cue to take their toy and play with you. It's a great way to bond with them.

THE "BED" COMMAND

This command should be done gently and with lots of love and praise. Just like your parents ask you to go to bed when it's time, you must train your puppy when it's time to sleep.

Step 1:

Guide your puppy to their bed.

Step 2:

Place a treat on the bed, but don't let them take it.

Step 3:

Allow them to get in the bed.

Step 4:

Say *"bed,"* reward with the treat, and praise them.

Of course, your puppy may get out of bed as soon as they eat the treat. If they do this, incorporate the stay command. Take a few tries with this, and your puppy will learn that *"bed"* means it's time to go to sleep.

THE "LEAD" COMMAND

It doesn't matter how small or big your puppy is; it may get tangled in its lead. When they are new to walking, this happens frequently and can be awkward and frustrating for both of you. So, how do you teach them to walk like a pro?

Step 1:

Wrap the lead gently into a loop around your puppy's paw.

Step 2:

Keep a treat in your hand.

Step 3:

Make the loop larger and pull the lead towards you as gently as possible.

Step 4:

Your puppy will naturally lift their paw, and the loop will come off.

Step 5:

As soon as this happens, say *"lead"* and reward.

Repeat this until your puppy knows that they have to lift their paw whenever you say *"lead."* When they do this, the tangles of their lead will come undone, and you can continue with your walk.

THE "SPEAK" COMMAND

This is another fun command. You can use it whenever you want your puppy to communicate with you, or if they are hiding somewhere in the house and you want to find them.

Step 1:

Watch your puppy closely and wait for them to bark.

Step 2:

When they bark, say *"speak"* loudly and give them a treat. Add praise and love.

This is something that you will need to be flexible with. Keep repeating the cue whenever your puppy barks, and soon, they will think that you saying *"speak"* means they must bark.

THE "QUIET" COMMAND

This is the opposite of *the "speak"* command, and your puppy needs to learn it. In case they are too loud, you can use it to quiet them.

Step 1:

Use the *"speak"* command and wait for them to bark.

Step 2:

When they bark, wait for them to quiet down.

Step 3:

As soon as they stop barking, add the verbal cue *"quiet."* Use your fingers to make a shhh sign in front of your lips. Be joyful when saying this so that your puppy doesn't think you are scolding them for doing something you asked them to do, i.e., speak!

Step 4:

Give them a treat and praise.

Both *"speak"* and *"quiet"* are flexible training techniques and can be taught as games. Just wait for your puppy to bark and begin playing with these commands; they'll understand soon enough.

THE "CAR" COMMAND

Some puppies love car rides. Making the car a comfortable space for them, with a puppy seat, toys, and treats, will make car journeys fun and memorable. So, have you thought of how to get your puppy into the car?

Step 1:

Keep your puppy on a long lead.

Step 2:

Have the door of your car open.

Step 3:

Place a treat on the area where you want your pup to sit.

Step 4:

Let them climb up, and as soon as they reach the desired spot, say *"car!"*

Step 5:

Let them have the treat.

You can practice this even when you're not going anywhere. Just keep your car door open and practice four to five times every day till your puppy knows that when you say *"car,"* they have to climb up and sit in the desired spot.

THE "HEEL" COMMAND

This is the final command we'll learn. It's a great way to make sure your puppy is disciplined during their walks and walks alongside you. Teaching heel involves training your dog to stay close to you when walking. You will need to be consistent in training.

Step 1:

Take your puppy for a walk. Choose either the right or left side you want to train your dog to walk with you. Choose only one side to training your dog and stick with that side.

Step 2:

Ask them to sit beside you by pointing either right or left side.

Step 3:

Take a treat and show it to your puppy.

Step 4:

As soon as they come to your chosen side, say "heel."

Keep practicing this command every five minutes in your walk, with increased time intervals before you give them the treat. They'll soon understand that *"heel"* means they have to sit quietly in your chosen space.

KEY POINTS

Well done for making it so far. You now have a trunk full of tricks to teach your puppy and bond with them. Before we move to the next chapter, here are some key things to remember.

- Be regular with practice sessions.
- Never include any negativity; always be smiling and loving, and reward liberally whenever your puppy is successful.
- The *"sit"* command will teach your puppy to sit in one place upon your verbal cue.
- The *"lie"* command will help you in making them lie down when you want.
- Teaching the *"come"* command will enable your puppy to come up to you.
- The *"no"* command will prevent them from doing something forbidden.
- The *"leave it"* command will teach them to leave something they shouldn't focus on.
- *"Stay"* will teach them to wait quietly in place.
- *"Get off"* will teach them to get down from a place, like a sofa or a counter.
- *"Watch me"* will help you get their attention when you want to distract them or help them focus.
- *"Wait"* will teach them not to jump on people who enter the house.
- *"Drop it"* will teach them to drop something.
- *"Handle your business"* will teach them the rules of being housebroken.
- *"Take it"* is a fun command that will help you play together.
- *"Bed"* will help them realize it is time for bed.
- *"Lead"* will train them to untangle lead knots when walking.

- *"Speak"* and *"quiet"* will train them to bark and be quiet upon your cues.
- *"Car"* will train them to get in the car with ease, and finally,
- *"Heel"* will train your puppy to walk in a disciplined way and pause when asked to.

4

FUN GAMES FOR YOUR PUPPY AND YOU!

Games are a wholesome means to bond with your puppy. Think of your puppy as a child who needs engagement. When you play with them, you not only make them feel involved and loved, you also end up having a lot of fun yourself.

You can play a variety of games with your puppy, inside and outside. Think of how many benefits your puppy will get from this. Enjoyment aside, they will be more active, have better mental coordination, and get to know you as a friend. The social and emotional well-being of your puppy rests on an active daily playtime routine. It also keeps them to get healthy and is a fun way to destress. The same applies to you. What a better way to destress than an hour with a little ball of love (*Why Playtime Is of the Utmost Importance for Your Dog*, 2021)? Let's get your puppy and you started.

INDOOR GAMES

Indoor games are a great way to engage your puppy if you are in isolation or cannot go out due to bad weather or any other problem. It's also a way to make sure they get their exercise without going out. Tiring your puppy out is important because otherwise, they will channel their energy in destructive ways. This can mean chewed-up sofa-ends, socks disappearing, and slippers getting decapitated. These are signs that your puppy is inventing their playtime because you are not engaging with them. The best way to prevent this chaos is to play with them.

FiND IT!

This is a great way to engage your puppy and so enjoyable to watch. In this game, you hide a toy/treat and signal for your puppy to find it.

Step 1:

Begin by showing your puppy a toy. Use an old toy that will already have its scent on it. Alternatively, show your puppy a treat.

Step 2:

Now, making sure they follow your movements and put the toy or the treat under a chair or table.

Step 3:

When your puppy goes to retrieve it, add the verbal cue *"find it!"*

Step 4:

When they retrieve it, reward them with praise. If you used a toy, give them a treat.

- Your puppy's playtime doesn't need to follow a timeline. You can play whenever you see they are getting bored or trying to get into trouble. But, make sure you take time out for playing every day.
- After repeating this, amp up the difficulty. Begin hiding the toy or the treat, and give the verbal cue.
- Your puppy will try to find the item or the treat by sniffing it out.

Once your puppy has become an expert at this game in one room, you can play with them in other house rooms too. This will keep the game fresh and also satisfy your puppy's curiosity. Breeds like golden retrievers particularly enjoy a good game of *"find it"* because, well, that's what they are meant to do.

To add another level to this game, you can also teach your puppy to find people.

Step 1:

Begin by asking your guardian or a friend to help out. There should be two of you.

Step 2:

Ask your guardian/friend to hide.

Step 3:

In the meantime, keep your puppy distracted.

Step 4:

When the other person has hidden, say *"find"* + *your guardian/friend's name.* So, say you have a friend called Heidi. Ask your puppy to *"find Heidi!"*

Step 5:

Keep repeating until your puppy locates them. This will take time since humans are not treats or toys, so you are essentially introducing a new training technique.

Step 6:

Your puppy will eventually find your guardian/friend. When they do, praise and reward them.

- Repeat, and say *"find + person's name"* every time you play so that your puppy eventually knows that when you say *"find"* with someone else's name, you are asking them to locate where they are.

Keep this simple when you start by asking your guardian or friend to hide in obvious places where your puppy can see them. Make sure your puppy already knows them because puppies identify the names of people they are familiar with. Remember to reward with lots of praise and attention. Increase the difficulty as your puppy gets used to the game.

FETCH!

Teaching your puppy to *"fetch"* may take some time, but they do catch on. Some puppies like to chase but don't retrieve. This means, when you throw a ball, they'll get it and hold it in their mouth instead of bringing it to you. Be patient with this exercise because it's a verbal command that they are not used to, so taking time is natural.

Step 1:

Begin by choosing a suitable toy. Don't get something too big or clunky; this will only confuse your puppy. Good toys to play fetch with include rubber balls, squeaky balls, discs, and rope toys.

Step 2:

If your puppy doesn't show interest, begin by running along with them. Throw the toy and begin running toward it. Your puppy will become interested and follow you. Once you reach the toy, pick it up and throw it again. Repeat this till you have your puppy's full attention.

Step 3:

Once you have their attention, throw the toy a little distance away. Your puppy will think you'll run after it, so they will run to catch it too. They will take it in their mouth.

Step 4:

Eventually, when they see you are not following, they will bring the toy to you.

Step 5:

When they do that, immediately say *"fetch,"* then praise and reward generously.

Don't be discouraged if this game takes some time. It's not an easy process for your puppy to understand what you want, so if you see them getting tired, pause and try the next day again.

THE SHELL GAME

The *Shell* game is an excellent tool for the mental stimulation of your puppy. It's a problem-solving game that will put your puppy's brain to work. We want that. The more functional and intelligent your puppy becomes, the healthier it will be.

Step 1:

Take three cups. These can be paper cups or small clay pots your puppy won't be able to knock over.

Step 2:

Begin with one cup/pot, and hide a treat under it.

Step 3:

Wait for your puppy to touch the pot with their nose. This will happen naturally.

- When this happens, reward the nose touch with lots of praise and give them the treat.
- When your puppy begins doing this constantly, add a command, like *"get it."*
- Next, before you give the treat, wait for your puppy to touch the pot with their paw. This will happen, eventually, because your puppy will get frustrated in trying to access the treat.
- At first contact with the paw, praise and reward your puppy.
- Keep doing this till your puppy constantly touches their paw to the pot. They should understand that doing this movement will fetch them a treat.
- Next, introduce a second pot.
- To begin with, just place it beside the pot with the treat in it. Don't move anything.
- Encourage your puppy to sniff the two pots and touch the correct one.

- When they do that, give them the treat and praise them lavishly.

Wait till your puppy becomes an expert with two pots, and then introduce a third. By keep practicing, you will be able to shuffle the pots, and your puppy should still locate the one with the treat in it.

WHiCH HAND?

The *"Which Hand"* game is a great one to play in conjunction with the *Shell* game. These games teach your puppy to identify scent better, which comes in handy later in life. All of us have distinct scents, and our puppies identify each of us based on how we smell to them.

Step 1:

Begin with one treat. For this game, you can make it more fun by switching dog treats with pieces of cut fruit like papaya, or an almond (make sure your puppy doesn't have nut-allergies first), or even a small piece of peeled apple.

Step 2:

Place the treat in one of your palms.

Step 3:

Let your puppy sniff the treat without letting them eat it.

Step 4:

Close your palms into fists, and hold them out in front of your puppy.

Step 5:

Let your puppy choose a fist.

Step 6:

If they choose wrong, don't lose patience. Wait for them to choose the right fist.

Step 7:

As soon as they do, open your fist, give them the treat, and say "*touch!*"

Step 8:

Repeat four to five times in one round.

With time, your puppy will realize that once they choose the fist with a treat in it, they'll get the treat. This is a neat little game to occupy their attention when you are physically tired and don't want to run around.

TUG OF WAR

Contrary to what many people think, playing tug of war does not make a puppy aggressive or disobedient. Rather, it engages them and allows them to feel happy. When you let your puppy win a game of tug of war, it makes them feel proud. It's a fun way to boost their confidence. It engages them physically and mentally, increases their attention span, and teaches them to be gentle with you.

- Begin by establishing the rules of the game. Some things should be penalized. For example, if your puppy's teeth touch your hand, say "*no*" immediately and stop playing.

They will understand that if they do this, you won't play with them anymore.

- Make sure your puppy is well trained with the *"sit," "take it," "drop it,"* and *"no"* commands. This will make it easy for you to control the game without seeming overbearing.
- Use a tug toy (like a tug-rope) that will be long enough to keep your puppy's teeth at a distance from your hands.
- The toy should be durable, or else it will tear during the game.
- Keep the toy away when you are not playing tug of war. This is a special toy reserved for this game.

Step 1:

Teach your puppy to grab the toy when you give them your permission. Hold the toy up or off to one side.

Step 2:

Say the verbal cue *"sit"* and wait for your puppy to sit down.

Step 3:

Once your puppy sits down, say, *"take it."*

Step 4:

Let your puppy grab the toy and gently move the tug from side to side, encouraging them to pull from the side opposite to the side you are holding.

Step 5:

Never pull the toy upwards; this can injure your puppy's neck or spine. Only move it back and forth and sideways.

Step 6:

Your puppy may become excited and begin to growl. This is normal and a way for you to understand they are enjoying the game.

Step 7:

If you find them becoming too excited, say *"drop it"* and take a breather.

If your puppy's teeth come in touch with your hand, immediately say *"no"* and stop the game.

Your puppy will eventually learn to play fair. They'll realize that the moment they become too excited or jumpy, you will stop playing. They don't want that. So, with time, they will engage in this game with the right amount of excitement. It's a great game to teach your puppy coordination and patience. Remember to let them win because this is a massive positive reinforcement for them. When they win, reward and praise, then say how wonderful and strong they are. You're raising your puppy's self-confidence.

CLEAN UP!

This is a handy trick to get your puppy to clean up after themselves. Believe me, puppies are messy in the most adorable way possible. They will litter a room with toys, and if they know this trick, you won't have to clean up after them all the time. It's also a great way to teach your puppy to obey you.

For this trick, your puppy will need to be familiar with the *"take it"* and *"drop it"* commands.

Step 1:

Keep a treat in your hand and call your puppy.

Step 2:

Point to a toy that is on the floor. Say *"take it."*

Step 3:

Go to their toy basket.

Step 4:

Show them the treat and wait for them to come with the toy.

Step 5:

If your puppy drops the toy immediately and runs to get the treat, don't lose hope. Don't give them the treat. Go back to the toy and repeat the command, making sure they can see the treat.

Step 6:

Wait till they approach the basket with the toy.

Step 7:

Say, *"drop it!"*

Step 8:

If they drop the toy in the basket, immediately say *"clean up"* and give them the treat. Make this a high-value treat, which will be something they love. This game isn't easy.

- Praise lavishly.
- Repeat a few times every day.

With enough practice, your puppy will associate the *"clean up"* command as a cue to pick their toys and put them in their basket. They will do it to earn your praise. When this phase comes, begin reducing the number of times you treat them. We have to keep your puppy healthy. Rely on praise and love.

OUTDOOR GAMES

Playing outdoors is essential for your puppy's development. It helps keep them mentally and physically fit while giving them a chance to get fresh air. Just like we don't like to stay within the four walls of our houses 24/7, our puppies also need some time outdoors.

Playing outdoors also helps your puppy spend their energy more efficiently. Since they have a bigger space to run in, they can tire themselves out faster. This is good news for you because when they come indoors, they'll be happily exhausted and won't worry about messing up your house. To ensure this, go for daily walks with your puppy, and add 20 minutes for just playtime outdoors (*Outdoor Games You Can Play With Your Puppy*, 2021).

FUN PUPPY TOYS FOR OUTDOOR ACTIVITIES

Before we talk about fun games, let's create an inventory of fun toys with which to engage your puppy outdoors.

- The classic ball is the most useful outdoor toy. You can play hours of fetch in the warm sun if you have a ball. You can get ones that come with squeakers inside and squeak them whenever your puppy comes close for amplified fun. Some balls also come with handles and can be used as tug toys too. Talk about variety.
- Whenever you are feeling lazy but want your puppy to get some exercise, get a ball launcher. These will launch balls in the air and send your puppy running for them. It's a life hack when you have tireless puppies.
- Get a variety of tug-of-war toys. Some of these come as ropes tied into a thick 'eight' shape. Some come with a

ball in the middle. Some come as long handles that you can hold on one side while your puppy holds the other. Whatever the variety, these serve multiple purposes. Not only will your puppy play tug-of-war with them, but they will also chew and teeth on them.
- Pullers are ring-shaped toys that work like tug-of-war toys. You hold one side, and your puppy holds the other. Let your puppy win a couple of times to boost their confidence.
- DIY agility courses (we'll talk about these in a second).

Now that you have a list of what you need let's get started.

AGILITY TRAINING

Agility training is an outdoor sport where you teach your puppy to go through a pre-set obstacle course within a time frame. Official courses generally have 14-20 obstacles. These include tunnels, weave poles, seesaws, jumps, and pause tables.

At pause tables, your puppy must stop for a set time. At each trial, your puppy and you race around the courses and hurdles. Your puppy does this by relying on your cues and body language. The connection this forges is stronger than cement.

If you are considering agility training, outdoor training is essential, and for this, you have to enroll your puppy in an agility class. Here's why agility training is excellent for your pup.

- Agility is one of the fastest-growing dog sports.
- It is an incredible way to exercise your puppy.
- It builds a deep relationship between you and your puppy.
- It's thrilling to watch your puppy go through tunnels, weave around poles, and leap through tires.

You can begin agility training for your pup in your house by setting obstacles in their path and rewarding them when they move around the obstacles to reach you. Once they are comfortable moving around these basic obstacles, take it outdoors. Make sure your puppy is well versed with all the training commands we covered in Chapter 2.

DIY WEAVE POLES

Weave poles are a great way to teach your puppy agility coursework in your backyard. It exercises their muscles, flanks, and joints.

You must take the help of your guardians in setting up this course.

- Make a course out of six *do-it-yourself* (DIY) poles. You can use your soccer cones or any other sturdy objects placed in a row. If you use buckets/gallon jars, fill them with sand or water so that they don't tip over.
- Keep enough space between each hurdle so that your puppy doesn't bump against them.
- Begin training by leading your puppy through the poles. Lead with a treat.
- Stay slightly ahead of your puppy and move the treat in the motion you want them to move.
- As your fur friend catches on, increase the speed. Begin with a very slow walk.
- Industry standards state that your poles should not be more than 24 inches apart. So, take the help of your guardians when setting these up.

DIY JUMP HURDLES

This exercise is a great way to maintain your puppy's joints and prevent their bones from becoming fragile. Jumping also helps to develop hindquarter muscles. Plus, your puppy will love it. Follow the below the steps to make the training easy.

- Begin by asking for the help of your guardians to set up the course.
- Look for something long and sturdy to use as a jumping rod. This can be the handle of a broom or a shovel, or even a shower curtain rod. To avoid injuries, encase the rod in a pool noodle.
- Take two chairs and set them outside with the help of your guardians.
- Set the rod on the rungs and secure it with duct tape. Better still, you can involve both your guardians and ask them to hold the rod from either end.
- A jumping hoop is another excellent option. You can make this with a hula hoop covered with a pool noodle and duct-taped between two chairs.
- Begin by keeping the rod or the hoop low. Coax your puppy through the hoop with a command. Keep trying till they get inside and come out. As soon as they do, add the verbal cue *"jump"* and praise and reward with a high-value treat.
- As soon as your puppy begins to understand what you want, raise the bars higher. Never raise it so high that they injure themselves.
- To find the maximum height which will be safe for your puppy, reach out to the local kennel club. They will also inform you about local groups that host agility courses for fun and games.

You can be very flexible and experiment with different agility courses in your backyard. If you want to compete in an agility race, it is great to enroll in a class and train. Be patient with agility training; it takes time and lots of effort from both your puppy and you. Remember, you are a team (*How to Create a DIY Agility Course in Your Backyard*, 2020).

SOCCER!

Soccer is a great way to engage your puppy and tire them out. Imagine the amount of fun you will have.

- Keep some treats ready.
- For this game, your puppy will need to know the *"watch me"* and *"leave it"* commands.
- Start by focusing your puppy's attention on a ball. Use a hard rubber ball of a bigger size than a tennis ball so that your pup won't take it in their mouth and bolt.
- If your puppy isn't looking at you, use the *"watch me"* command. As soon as you have their attention, praise and give a treat.
- Make sure the ball is within your reach. Your puppy should not have complete control over it.
- Gently nudge the ball with your foot, and wait for your puppy to respond.
- When your puppy nudges the ball with their nose or paw, praise and reward with a treat immediately (Cooper, 2019).

You will soon have an enthusiastic puppy nudging the ball around to get treats and praise. Amp it up and nudge the ball further away after practicing a few times. If your puppy gets too excited at any time, use *"leave it."* This should make them leave the ball and come directly to you for your praise.

HiDE AND SEEK

This is such a fun game. It's also a perfect way to bond with your puppy and teach them to be more familiar with their name and your voice.

- To begin, you will need the help of a guardian or a friend.
- Your puppy must have a basic idea of its name. We've read about how you can achieve this.
- Ask your guardian/friend to restrain your puppy.
- You go and hide behind a tree or a bush.
- Once you are ready, signal your guardian/friend to release your puppy and call out their name.
- Believe it or not, puppies know what their humans sound like intimately.
- They will identify you through your scent and voice.
- When they find you, act excited and surprised, then praise them liberally. Give them a treat too.

There's no time frame for the number of times you can play this game. Play till your puppy is appropriately tired, but not too much. You can also switch it up by asking your guardians or friends to hide the next time. Eventually, this game will help your puppy be completely familiar with their name as well.

Remember, the more you play with your puppy, the happier and healthier they will be. It's your way of telling them that you care and that you will do things to engage and excite them. Puppies thrive on attention and positive reinforcements, so always be kind, happy, and loving.

KEY POINTS

Before we get into the next chapter, here are some key points for you to remember.

- Games are important when bonding with your puppy.
- Games help develop your puppy's mental abilities and make them healthy and fit.
- When you don't want to go outdoors, you can engage your puppy in varied games indoors.
- *"Find it", "fetch", "shell", "tug-of-war"* and *"clean-up"* are great indoor games.
- Outdoor games will keep your puppy happy and help tire them out, so they don't display their discontent and make your house a mess.
- You can make DIY agility courses (like poles and jump hoops) to teach agility to your puppy.
- You can also play *soccer* and *hide-and-seek*.
- Always reward your puppy with a lot of love and praise.
- Let your puppy win in the tug of war games because this will boost their confidence.

Gosh, how fun was that? You know so much by now, and I cannot wait for you to have the best time playing with your puppy. Just a minute. Don't you want your puppy to be more clever and agile? Read on to learn how.

CLEVER DOG - TIPS AND TRICKS TO MAKE YOUR PUPPY SUPER CLEVER

By now, you are already a pro when it comes to knowing how to train your puppy. If your puppy develops more intelligence, they will follow all of your commands with ease and efficiency. So, are there any tricks you can teach to increase intelligence? Yes! Seeing how your puppy reacts to different training tricks is one of the most rewarding things about having them around. The joy and curiosity on their face make it worth our time. Before we start, remember that no two puppies are the same, so let yours learn in their own time. Be kind and happy so that it is a fun experience for both of you.

These tricks work best if your puppy has gone through the basic training stages, knows how to perform simple tasks, and can answer their name.

SHAKE HANDS

This is a handy little trick (pun intended). It's not just wholesome to have your puppy put their paw in your hand, but it also helps when you want to wash a muddy paw or trim their nails. Your puppy should know how to respond to their name and to sit upon command before you begin this trick.

Step 1:

Keep a few treats ready.

Step 2:

Call your puppy by their name.

Step 3:

Once they come to you, give the verbal cue "sit."

Step 4:

Once they sit down, take a treat and show it to them before hiding it in a closed fist. Don't give it to your puppy yet.

Step 5:

Hold out your fist with the palm facing upwards. Keep it at your puppy's chest level.

Step 6:

Wait till your puppy instinctively paws at your fist to get the treat.

Step 7:

When they do this, open your hand, and say the verbal cue "shake."

Step 8:

Let them have the treat.

- Praise and tell them what a good puppy they are.
- Repeat this process until your puppy symbolizes "shake" by pawing your fist to get a treat.
- Once they understand it, repeat all the previous steps, but without a treat in hand in front of your puppy.
- Say "shake."
- When your puppy paws your fist, give them a treat from the opposite fist (the one that is not in front of your puppy). Praise liberally.

Your puppy will begin to think that the verbal cue means they have to paw your fist. If they do that, you will love and praise them. It becomes a positive reinforcement and a way to get their attention. Gradually phase out the treat and use the verbal cue only.

CROSS YOUR PAWS

This is a cute trick! It's a great one to engage your pup when both of you are too tired to play anything else, and it's a fun one to teach. Your puppy will need to be familiar with their name and the "sit," "lie down," and "stay" commands.

Step 1:

Keep a treat in your hand.

Step 2:

Call your puppy, and once they come to you, ask them to "sit."

Step 3:

Now, gently go through the other motions. Ask them to lie down, and with the "stay" command, make them stay in that position.

Step 4:

Now, make a fist with your hand (the one with the treat in it).

Step 5:

Keep this closed fist in front of your puppy, at level with their paw.

Step 6:

Wait till they touch their paw to your hand.

Step 7:

Begin this with one hand and paw. For this explanation, let's say you place the treat towards their right paw with your right hand. Once they paw it, give them the treat and praise.

Step 8:

Next, move your fist with another treat. This time, keep it in the center, between the two paws of your puppy. Wait till they paw, and give them the treat. Remember to keep praising.

Step 9:

Next, repeat the motion, but instead of putting your fist in the center, keep it on top of your puppy's other paw (if you began with the right paw, this would mean keeping it on top of their left paw).

Step 10:

For this motion, remember to keep it on top and not in front of their paw. It's different from the first movement where you kept your fist in front, not on it.

Step 11:

Wait till they paw you with their right paw (if you placed your fist on top of their left paw). When they do this, praise and reward.

Step 12:

Now, slowly move your fist with another treat and bring it to the left paw side. Wait till they paw with their right hand. If they get confused, pause and repeat the whole process. Repeat until they understand they have to paw with their right hand. At one stage, they will do it as an impulse.

Step 13:

When they get it right, they will be crossing their paws. As soon as your puppy crossed their right paw over their left paw to get to your fist, say "cross," and shower your praise on them. Reward with the treat.

Repeat these steps until they become familiar with it.

This may be a little confusing to begin with. But don't worry, you will get there. Gradually phase out the treats and use the verbal cue "cross" to get them to cross their paws. This is such a pleasure to watch. It's a great exercise for your puppy's brain development, so be patient while teaching them.

DOUBLE-CROSS PAWS

As the name suggests, this is a variant of the "Cross" trick. So, before teaching your puppy to do this, make sure they are familiar with crossing one paw over the other.

Step 1:

Call your puppy, and once they come, ask them to sit and then lie down.

Step 2:

Make sure they stay in that position.

Step 3:

With a treat in your hand, ask your puppy to cross their paws.

Step 4:

Because your puppy is already familiar with the trick, they will cross one paw over the other (if they learned it with the right paw, they will cross the right one over the left).

Step 5:

Once they do that, give them their treat and praise.

Step 6:

Now, go through all the motions of the "cross" trick, but this time, do it with the opposite hand and paw (in this case, the left hand and left paw).

Step 7:

As soon as your puppy's left paw crosses their right paw, say "change" and give them the treat. Praise liberally.

Practice this motion four to five times, then amp it up. Once your puppy is familiar with the "change" command, alternate between "cross" and "change."

This trick may confuse your puppy, to begin with, because they are transitioning from one limb to another. If you find that they get frustrated, stop. It's not good to make them feel like they do not understand you. Give them a break, making sure to look happy and loving. Play something else. Once your puppy feels happy again, come back and try this trick. When they get the hang of it, remember to phase out the treats slowly. At this stage, they should put one paw over the other with the "cross" and "change" commands.

FiND THE TREASuRE!

Some puppies are natural diggers, and they will burrow into the ground with any opportunity they get. If your puppy belongs to this group, don't encourage this behavior further because they'll dig up your whole house. If, however, they don't do this, you can teach them to dig as a fun way to get to their treat. It will engage them mentally and won't require too much effort from your side.

Step 1:

Begin by placing a high-value treat under a towel.

Step 2:

Make sure your puppy watches you do this.

Step 3:

Wait till your puppy begins to paw the towel to retrieve the treat.

Step 4:

Don't say anything until they use their paws. If they nudge with their nose, say "no."

- Eventually, your puppy will begin to paw the towel to get to the treat.
- When they do this, say "dig," move the towel, let them take the treat, and praise them.

You can play this in different rooms of your house. After they get familiar, change it up. Begin hiding treats under a pile of leaves in your yard, and ask them to dig. They'll have so much fun burrowing through the leaves to get to the treat. As always, be patient and consistent, and gradually phase out the treat.

RiNG THE BELL!

This is a handy trick. It can make housebreaking your puppy so much easier. Here's what you have to do.

Step 1:

Repeat this trick once in the morning after your puppy wakes up and once at night before they go to bed.

Step 2:

Practice this outside in the spot where they do their business

Step 3:

Keep a treat in your hand.

Step 4:

Ask your puppy to sit.

Step 5:

Make a fist with this hand and bring it to shoulder level with your puppy.

Step 6:

Say "paw."

Step 7:

When your puppy touches your fist with their paw, give them the treat and praise.

Step 8:

Next, hang a small bell from your hand.

Step 9:

Repeat the verbal cue "paw" and wait till they ring it.

Step 10:

Add the verbal cue you use to ask them to do their business. They should already be familiar with what this means.

Step 11:

Once your puppy is done, reward and treat them.

Gradually move this trick indoors. Your puppy will begin to look at the bell as a way to tell you they need to go.

Keep the bell in one place where your puppy can see and access it every day. This trick will take time. Remember to begin this outside and then practice indoors. This will help them understand the significance of the bell. We've discussed how to use verbal commands for housebreaking your pup earlier, so go back for a refresher if you need to, and then teach them this neat trick.

SPiN AROUND

Teaching your puppy to spin around can make them a hit at social gatherings. Imagine how fun it will be for your friends and family to watch them spin upon your command and how proud you will feel.

Step 1:

Keep a treat ready.

Step 2:

Hold the treat in your hand, and move it over your puppy's head in a circular motion, letting their head follow your hand's movement.

Step 3:

Keep going in the circular motion, and pause just behind your puppy's head.

Step 4:

Wait for them to turn around to take the treat.

Step 5:

As soon as they do, say "spin!" and give them the treat.

Step 6:

Practice this four to five times and praise liberally each time they turn to take the treat.

Gradually increase the number of spins you make your puppy do.

Spinning will take some time to perfect since it's not a normal movement for your puppy. Once they can complete a few successful circles, phase out the treats, and make them follow your hand movements, then your verbal cue alone. Take your time, and don't overdo it.

SAY BYE!

This is a very cute trick to say goodbye to your guests. Your puppy should be familiar with basic training commands at this point, like how to "shake."

Step 1:

Keep a treat ready.

Step 2:

Call your puppy, and ask them to sit.

Step 3:

Ask your puppy to "shake." When they lift their paw to shake your hand, move your hand up slightly so that they have to move their paw up to get to your hand.

Step 4:

When they do this, praise and give them a treat.

Step 5:

Repeat this motion a few times. Each time, move your hand a little higher until your puppy is raising their paw near their head level.

Step 6:

Once your puppy has done this successfully several times, add the verbal cue "wave." Next, as soon as your puppy begins lifting their paw, say "wave," and only give them the treat when they raise their paw near or above their head.

Praise and be happy when giving the command. Make sure they see how pleasantly surprised you are.

Your puppy will soon learn to wave upon command. Many puppies will lift their paws instinctively to reach the treat. If yours doesn't, simply keep practicing till they associate lifting the paw near or above their heads with getting the treat and the verbal cue, plus lots of love. Once they get to this stage, begin phasing out the treat and rely on praise and verbal cue.

HiGH FiVE!

This is a super-fun trick to engage your puppy and impress your guests. To learn this, your puppy must be familiar with basic training tricks. The good news is, this works more or less the same way as the "shake" command, so if they know how to shake, they'll get here in no time.

Step 1:

Keep a treat in your hand.

Step 2:

Now, call your puppy, and ask them to sit down.

Step 3:

As soon as they sit, bring your hand into a fist (with the treat in it), and place this at nose-level with your puppy.

Step 4:

Say "shake."

Step 5:

Wait till your puppy raises their paw to take your fist and open your hand, making sure to hold the treat between your thumb and index finger.

Step 6:

As soon as your puppy touches your open hand, say "high five!"

Step 7:

Give your puppy the treat, and praise them for being such a clever puppy.

Repeat this consistently till your puppy associates the open palm and the verbal cue "high five" with touching their paw to your palm. They will get the hang of it. When they do, rely on the hand gesture and command, and phase out the treat.

For all of these commands, always be ready to stop and try later if your puppy gets tired. These games are based on mental stimulation, requiring more than just running around to fetch a ball. It requires your puppy to be in one place and think about what you want. It's meant to be confusing for a kid. Be loving and steady, and you will be rewarded in time (Wall, 2021).

KEY POINTS

Wasn't this so much fun? Intelligence will be vital in enabling your puppy to think and learn. It's not just about being clever. The more they learn to think, the more obedient they become. This, in turn, makes them sociable. So, before we move on, here are some key points for you to remember.

This section covers tips and tricks to increase your puppy's intellectual stimulation.

- Always keep treats ready. Use high-value treats for these exercises.
- It is not in your puppy's nature to be still for an extended period, so be patient if they potter off. Try again another time.
- "Shake" will teach your puppy to shake their paw with your hand.
- "Cross" will train them to cross one paw with the other.
- "Change" will work on getting them to cross the opposite paw.

- "Cross" and "change" together will help them cross one paw over the other and repeat the same motion with the other paw.
- "Wave" will teach them to raise their paw near or above their head.
- "High-five" will teach them to raise their paw to your palm in a high-five motion.

Well done for getting this far. Now that we've gone through all the fun and games, let's take a moment to consider some mistakes we make while training puppies and how we can avoid them.

COMMON
TRAINING
MISTAKES

You've just begun training your puppy, and you find that they won't listen to you. They get tired, they do things you ask them not to, and they are stubborn. You feel that you can't take it anymore.

Please don't. It's not your fault, and neither is it your puppy's. Here's a simple thing- your puppy is not a human. They don't speak or function in the same manner or with the same language. So, think of an example- your mother tongue is English, but you have begun learning Spanish. Will you be an expert in a month? No! You need time, patience, and practice, right? It's no different for your puppy.

With this in mind, let's run through some common mistakes many of us make when we take on a puppy. I made my share of these mistakes, so trust me, you are not alone.

WAITING TOO LONG TO TRAIN YOUR PUPPY

Begin training your puppy the day they come home with you, irrespective of their age. Don't wait for them to grow older, because this will mean they grow old with no idea of how to behave. They will naturally do whatever comes to their mind. The only way to curb this is to begin when they set foot in your house. The ultimate goal of training your puppy is to shape and form their behavior to suit human society, and you don't have to wait for them to grow old to begin that.

Indeed, you won't begin advanced training till they are about four to six months old, but basic training and housebreaking your pup is a must in the early stages. These won't just discipline them; they will also help forge a deeper bond between the two of you. When the time for advanced training comes, they will find it easier to trust you and follow your movements and commands. This will make challenging training sessions, like agility sessions, far more comfortable for both of you.

INADEQUATE TRAINING

Training your puppy cannot begin and end in one day. It isn't a one-time thing; rather, it needs daily revision and practice.

The best results will come when you train your puppy every day, even after they master a trick or cue. Choose one thing at a time, and hold short sessions spread through the day. This will make it fun while keeping your puppy engaged. It will help them develop obedience and regularity. When you move to advanced training, remember to return to the basics once in a while.

Your puppy will never stop learning because they imbibe and internalize cues from their environment. So, if your environment is unresponsive, they will be sad. To prevent this, let them feel like you are making an effort to involve and train them.

BEiNG RiGiD AND IMPATiENT

No two puppies are alike. Even among the same breeds, there will be minute differences in behavior. So, instead of taking a *"one-size-fits-all"* approach, be flexible with your pup. Try different plans and see what makes your puppy (and you) happiest.

- This includes trying different training styles and joining a few classes before you narrow down upon one. So, while you shouldn't give up if one kind of class or training method doesn't work, also don't try to force it on your pup. Look for another approach; try another day, and you will find the right fit for both of you.

- Every puppy will learn differently. Try your utmost best not to get angry or frustrated if they can't catch on to something. This will make things worse because your puppy will become frightened and upset and withdraw, thinking that you don't love them anymore.

Rather, consider some things like:

- Has the training session been going on for too long? Each session should be no longer than 15 minutes. If you find your puppy's attention wavering, check the time. If it feels like it's gone on too long, wrap it up.

- Did you end the session with praise and love? Your puppy just did what you asked them to. Did you show them how proud you are?

- Is the trick too complicated? If yes, consider breaking it down into smaller tricks, and teach them one component at a time. There's no rush.

- Are you tired? Here's an example of what can happen. You ask your puppy to sit. They don't do that. In a wave of frustration, you keep asking them to sit until they do it. Then, you give them a treat. This is you telling your puppy that your command is just a suggestion, and they can wait to sit till you repeat it five times, or 50. Instead, say the command once. Wait for them to give you their response. If they don't, repeat after a two-minute break.

CALLING YOUR PUP FOR AN UNPLEASANT TASK

Say you were in trouble for getting into mischief. Would you like to go if your guardian was calling you, knowing that you're about to get a scolding? Of course not! It's the same for your puppy.

- When you call your puppy by their name and associate that with something they don't like, such as going to the vet or getting their nails trimmed, their name will cause a negative reaction in them. As a result, they will stop approaching you when you call them, and worse, they may hide.

- Instead of associating their name with something negative, go to them when you must carry out a task they will not like. Sit beside them, give them a treat, and praise them liberally. Let them know what a good puppy they are. Then slowly, take them with you.

- Never approach them in an angry state of mind. They will not learn anything if you punish or shout at them, so try your best not to be harsh. Calm yourself if they have made a mistake. They probably don't know what they did wrong. Once you are calm, go to them, point to the error, and gently say *"no."* With time, they will get the hang of it.

LOSiNG YOUR TEMPER WiTH STUBBORN PUPPiES

This is a mistake most of us make. Puppies tire out easily, and sometimes, they like being naughty. We're trying hard to teach them a trick, but they will not listen. So, we get mad and yell at them. That's a mistake. It will make things harder for your puppy because they don't understand why you react with anger. Instead, if you find them getting distracted, stop the session, and try after an hour or two.

WHAT TO REMEMBER

- One step at a time. Before you start a new trick, revisit an old one. It's always good, to begin with, something your puppy already knows, like asking to sit or lie. Reward each positive action, regardless of how small the success. This will help your puppy associate training as a rewarding process.

- Control your puppy's environment. Take precautions to guarantee their full attention. This includes choosing the right spot for conducting training sessions. There should be good light and ventilation, and be free from distractions. If you are training outside, always keep a lead on your puppy. Even a squirrel will be enough to distract them.

- Be consistent. Make sure that your family is in the loop with your training schedule. So, if you use the *"sit"* command to train your puppy to sit, and your guardian uses a different command, that will create a lot of confusion. Ensure that all of you are on the same page.

POTTY-TRAINING ISSUES

Housebreaking a puppy is a full-time job, and you need your guardians' help while doing this. Even with this, initial slip-ups will happen. There can be several reasons for this, including a communication gap or your puppy not being able to control themselves. Some common mistakes happen, and knowing them will help you tackle potty training easier (Schade, 2017).

- Skipping crate training is a mistake. They will not develop restraint or bladder control and go about without discipline. If you keep them in a crate, they will learn to treat it as their home, a place that they must keep clean. This will teach them to wait and give a cue if they want to do their business.

- Don't let your puppy roam freely without supervision. They have little bladder control when they are young, and if left to their own devices, they will relieve themselves wherever they find fit. So, to prevent this, keep an eye on your puppy all the time. This is essential for the first two months because the housebreaking habits that they learn will stay with them forever. If you need a break from supervision, involve your parents.

- Don't take your puppy's gestures for granted. They are trying to tell you something. If they are going around in circles, or nervously pawing the door, or sniffing a spot, it probably means they need to go. We often mistake this as a display of cuteness, but it's a call to be let out.

- Sometimes, we forget to praise our puppies after displaying good behavior, like doing their business in the right spot. This is a mistake because now they think it doesn't make a difference where they go. Instead, if you give them a treat and tell them what a good job they did, they will likely repeat the same action in the future.

- We make the mistake of overestimating the hold-capacity of our puppies. An active three-month-old puppy will probably have bladder control for three hours at a time and no more (Schade, 2017). On the other hand, if they are asleep, they may hold it a little longer. The key is always to be aware and on the lookout for signals.

- If you are taking your puppy outside and just waiting for them to do their job without a verbal cue, that's a big mistake. You must add a command when they do their business, like *"good potty."* Remember that this is training, and no training works without a command.

- Finally, never make the mistake of punishing for accidents. They happen, and we get annoyed because our expectations let us down. But, if you get angry, your puppy will think they have made a grave error and become sad and depressed. We don't want that. Be kind and forgiving because they will respond much better to love than to harshness.

ACCEPTING THE WHYS

Before moving on, let's talk about some whys- why is my puppy biting me? Why is my puppy chewing my furniture?

WHY IS MY PUPPY BITING ME?

Puppy mouthing is normal behavior. This is particularly prone to happen when they are teething (losing their baby teeth). Keep enough chew toys ready. The only time you should be concerned is if a puppy bites you out of fear or when you are trying to train them. This is a signal that you've pushed too hard, and you need to take it easy. Consider enrolling your puppy in a behavior class if it helps. A trained professional will guide you through this process (*Mouthing, Nipping and Biting in Puppies*, 2021). However, if you see sudden aggression with biting behavior, you need to see a vet since sometimes a dog exhibits pain or other medical symptoms through behavioral changes.

WHY IS MY PUPPY PEEING SO MUCH?

Young puppies generally pee more. However, if there is a sudden increase, this can be for several reasons. Your puppy may be trying to mark their territory, or they may be showing their anxiety by peeing. This means you are training or disciplining too much, and you need to take it down a notch. On the other hand, they may see you after school, get extremely happy, and pee. This is a happy reaction. On a serious level, if you notice a sudden change in urination patterns, always consult with your guardians and your family vet (Harris, 2021).

WHY IS MY PUPPY BITING THE FURNITURE?

The simple answer is your puppy likes it. The furniture gives their mouth something to chew on, and they are channeling their boredom. This is a signal that they need more engagement and exercise. I can never overemphasize the importance of having chew toys in the house. If you see your puppy do this, don't scold them. Give the verbal cue *"leave it,"* reward when they do, and engage them in a constructive activity.

WHY IS MY PUPPY REFUSING TO EAT?

There is absolutely nothing to be worried about if your puppy refuses to eat on their first day in your home. They are in a new environment, and it will take some time for them to adjust to it. However, if the lack of appetite persists, it can be because of a digestive issue, so consult with your family vet and get medical advice.

 **KEY POINTS**

Kudos for coming this far! Now, you know some common mistakes all of us make as new owners. It took me time to adjust too! So, you are not alone. Here are some key points to look over.

- You and your puppy are on this journey together.
- Never be harsh or angry with your puppy.

- Don't wait too long before beginning training. Begin training your puppy from the day they come to your house. Begin with the simple things.
- Be regular with your sessions.
- Never force them to perform a task.
- Involve your family in training sessions to maintain consistency.
- Take your time and have patience while housebreaking your pup.
- Be on the lookout for signals like walking in circles, sniffing a spot, or pawing the door.
- Always use a verbal command when your puppy does their business.
- If your puppy bites you when you are training, consider taking a break.
- Keep chewing toys around the house.
- Engage your puppy in an activity if you see them chewing the furniture.
- Always consider the advice of your family vet.

Overall, I truly believe that we learn as we go. You have gained a friend for life. This friend will love you unconditionally. What can you do in return? Make sure that they have a healthy, happy, and wholesome life. Of course, mistakes will happen! But, what is important is how you deal with those mistakes and how you work through them *together*. You and your puppy will be the best team ever. All you have to do is take some time to get to know them and train them.

HOW TO CARE FOR YOUR PUPPY

We're almost at the home stretch! You already know so much to help you bond, connect, and form an everlasting relationship with your puppy.

It's important to remember that having a puppy goes beyond the cute pictures we see on social media platforms. Sure, puppies are adorable! But, they are living, breathing creatures who need care and upkeep. So, in this section, we'll cover the basics of how you can care for your pup. Please remember that primary care should be given by your guardians because this includes technical and veterinarian assistance and vaccinations. But, you should be there by their side as much as you can.

SETTiNG UP A SuPPORT SYSTEM

This is a basic thing to do before your puppy comes home. A lot of us think we will do things as and when required, but when it comes to domesticating puppies, or any animals, it's a bad idea. It's always handy to be prepared.

- Make sure your whole family is on the same page. Teamwork is essential when it comes to taking on a new family member. You will need your guardians' help on many occasions.

- Keep a few numbers handy. These include the contacts of a reliable vet, an animal hospital, a pet salon, a dog walker, a doggy day-care, and a groomer.

- Let your close circle of friends and family know that you are getting a new family member. This should include close friends and relatives.

- Seek the help of your family members and friends in setting up the house before your puppy arrives. Do research on the appropriate crates, toys, bedding, and food.

Everything is more fun when your loved ones are involved. So, don't shy away from asking for help. Rather, feel proud about it because you are doing what is best for your puppy. A family that works together generates much more love and acceptance.

PuPPY PROOFiNG YOuR HOuSE

Your puppy will be the Christopher Columbus of your house. Puppies love exploring new places. When they enter your house, it is a whole new world of adventure that they must sniff and paw to make sense of. So, do both of you a favor, and devote some time to installing preventative puppy proofing. This will keep your furniture and other fragile items intact while also protecting your puppy from accidents.

Let your guardians take care of the puppy-proofing around the house. Parents, here's what you have to do.

- Keep all electric cords covered

- Tie up window cords and curtains, and make sure your puppy won't get entangled in them.

- Put toxic cleaning chemicals and supplies and disinfectants in higher cabinets.

- Invest in a tall, heavy-base trash can with a lid, which your puppy won't be able to knock over. Believe me; they will try.

- Purchase a crate for crate training, or invest in a baby gate to keep your puppy in a small space where the floors are washable. Use this space for the first two months until your puppy is completely housebroken.

- Don't give your puppy old shoes or stuffed animals to play with. Get proper puppy toys from a pet store so that they can differentiate between what belongs to them and what is yours. Train them to leave things that do not belong to them, or else they will never know the difference between their rubber ball and your Gucci belt.

- Don't let them get away with naughty behavior because of their cuteness or small size. Establish your routines clearly, because the older they get, the harder it will be to break a bad habit.

The key to puppy-proofing your house is to look at it from the perspective of a small human being. *What could hurt them? Where could they slip or fall? Are the stairs in need of being gated? Should we ward off the carpeted area?* Ask yourself all the necessary questions.

INTRODUCING YOUR PUPPY TO YOUR FAMILY

Bringing your puppy home is truly exciting! As a new puppy parent, you must remember that this is the beginning of an incredible journey full of many changes for your family and your puppy. Your puppy will be in a whole new environment with new sounds, smells, and a new family to love.

- Let your guardian be involved in introducing your puppy to members of the house.

- Place your puppy on a gentle lead, and allow them to roam in their new environment. Keep the lead in your hand and walk with them.

- Your puppy should feel comfortable but not be left alone for too long. They will get confused and overwhelmed and may have accidents.

- Introduce your family to your puppy one by one.

- Let your puppy go up to each member. Your puppy will sniff and paw them, and once they establish familiarity, ask each member to pat and praise your puppy gently. Don't rush this stage.

- Never underestimate the importance of crate training. It is an easy way to raise a disciplined, obedient puppy. Think of the crate as your puppy's bedroom, and train them to treat it as such.

- When exercising your puppy, keep them on a short lead unless you are training a command that requires a long one. Do not allow your puppy to pull or lead you. You need to establish yourself as the alpha or the dominant one. Otherwise, that cute little face will end up controlling all your activities. Knowing who is dominant will help them learn obedience.

- Begin socializing your puppy at 12 weeks. This will make things easier as they grow. Provide positive reinforcement when they behave well in front of guests and never allow them to jump at the sight of new people.

- By the time when your puppy is around four to six months old, consider enrolling them in obedience school. This will help with their socialization.

Finally, fill all your interactions with love. Your puppy will understand praise, treats, and love, most of all. Whether you are training them or playing with them, always rely on positive reinforcements.

DEVELOPING A GOOD FEEDING SCHEDULE

Always rely on high-quality food when it comes to feeding your puppy. Puppies have very sensitive stomachs, and some breeds are particularly prone to digestive issues.

- Never go for the cheaper items on the shelves because they may come with fillers and additives that will harm your puppy in the long run.

- If you are unsure of which brand of puppy food to pick, consult with your veterinarian to see what they recommend.

- Choose one brand and see if it suits your puppy's tummy. If it does, you have found the right fit. Stick to this brand. Switching brands too often can upset your little friend's tummy. If you wish to switch, consult with your vet before you decide.

- You should control the amount of food you give to your puppy. But keep their water bowl filled with fresh, clean water at all times.

- Remember that puppies will need more food than adult dogs because of their rapidly growing bodies.

- Based on this, your puppy should have four meals a day at eight to twelve weeks of age, three meals at three to six months, and two meals a day at six to twelve months.

Small or miniature breed puppies may need more frequent meals because of their blood sugar discrepancies. Consult with your vet to set up a proper feeding schedule for them (Mckeeby, 2018).

WHAT NOT TO FEED A PUPPY

Puppies are experts at manipulation. Don't get fuddled by those cute puppy dog eyes. They make them so that they can get their way around you. It is very hard to resist when your puppy comes up to you as you are eating dinner, with a sweet face and those big, pleading eyes. But, hard as it may be, you should avoid feeding scraps from the table to your puppy. It's a bad habit that should not be encouraged. Other than that, your puppy should never be allowed access to these food items.

- Never let your puppy have chocolate. Theobromine is a caffeine-like molecule that exists in chocolate. Dogs have enormous difficulty processing this, and for this reason, chocolate can be poisonous for them.

- Grapes and raisins can be fatal for puppies and dogs and may even cause renal failure. Avoid them at all costs.

- Chicken bones are a risky deal. While the nutrients are fine, they can splinter and injure your puppy's stomach and throat. This may cause serious injuries. So it's best to avoid them.

- If you want to feed your puppy raw meals, please do so only after taking instruction from nutritionists and the vet.

- Do not feed your puppy processed sugar. Dogs are at risk of high blood sugar and diabetes, and refined sugar contributes to this.

- Don't rely on high-fat food items because puppies are prone to gaining weight very quickly. This includes high-fat meat products like bacon, which also contain excessive salt.

- Avoid milk and other various milk products. They can cause diarrhea in your puppy and provoke allergies.

- Garlic and other members of the *allium* family, including onions, have a component called *thiosulfate,* which is toxic to dogs, but not humans. They can cause oxidative damage and anemia in dogs and must be avoided.

- Finally, avoid caffeine. It is toxic for your puppy and can damage their stomach and nerves.

When you are shopping for your puppy, keep a list of food items ready. Read labels carefully, and always get some high-value treats to reward and train them.

WHAT DOES MY PUPPY NEED?

So, now you may be wondering what products are essential for your fur-friend. The aisles of pet stores are always packed, and you may or may not need all you see. You find a costly but cute toothbrush and take it home, only to have your puppy chew it to shreds. Here's an essential bit of advice- *"Just because a dog food company made it, it doesn't mean that it's good for your dog"* (Mckeeby, 2018). Many companies will put their profits ahead of your puppy's wellbeing, and while this is sad, it's a harsh truth. Talk to your vet, and buy useful products. These include

- Two bowls, one for food and one for water.
- A sturdy leash and comfortable collar.
- Identification tags.
- A crate, pillow, and blanket.
- Small puppy treats.

- A good quality puppy food that is relevant to their age and weight.
- A bristle comb.
- A non-toxic, gentle puppy shampoo.
- A flea and tick comb.

Remember that your puppy will develop only as well as you allow them to. They need care, attention, and constant supervision. It's a hands-on job, and once you take the responsibility, it's also equally rewarding. So, take time for your preparations. We don't achieve success in something if we jump into it with zero planning. We spend months studying and revising till we perfect it. It's no different when you open your home and hearts to a new family member (Mckeeby, 2018).

CARING FOR A NEWBORN PUPPY

This is an exceptional situation. If you get your puppy from a breeder, try not to get one younger than two months. Puppies younger than this need to nurse from their mother to stay safe and healthy. In case you don't have an option, here are some tips to help you through. The instructions and tips in this section are for the parents since you have to take primary supervision when caring for a newborn puppy.

FEEDING A NEWBORN PUPPY

If you are taking care of a newborn puppy, be extra careful with their feeding. It is best to take the help of your vet.

- Firstly, brand new puppies need protection from germs. This protection comes through antibodies in their mother's milk during the initial stage of nursing. Dog mommies produce a milky-textured substance called *colostrum* which is what wards off infections in puppies.

- For this reason, it is imperative to let your puppy nurse from their mother as long as possible. If that is not a possibility, contact your vet immediately to find appropriate substitutes and supplements. You need them to ensure your puppy's survival.

- After the first few weeks, puppies that cannot nurse can be fed by you through other methods. Take the advice and recommendation of your vet before you begin. If your puppy has trouble nursing from a bottle, you may need to look for alternatives such as a stomach tube. Purchase a formula that is made for canines.

- Feed your puppy while they lie on their stomach. Other positions may cause them to choke. Don't use a microwave, instead place the bottle in a cup of warm water. If you feel a slight warmth after putting a bit of the warmed milk on your skin, the milk is warm enough.

- Once your puppy has fed, pat them gently on their back. This will help them burp up any air that they may have swallowed during feeding.

FEEDING SCHEDULE

Newborn puppies need to be constantly fed every two to three hours. So, you'll be as busy with them as you would be with a newborn human.

- If you are making the feeding formula, follow package instructions on how much to mix. Make a note of whether that feels enough for your puppy.

- Puppies need a warm environment for sleeping and eating. This is because their body temperature isn't self-regulated during the first few weeks of their life. If they are cold, it's not a good sign because they will not digest their food properly. To prevent this, keep a heat source, like a hot water bag, under a towel or blanket in their nesting box. Place it next to a cool area so that they can move there if it gets too hot.

- You may notice some signs like your puppy biting or chewing their feeding bottle at about three to four weeks. This is a signal for you to start soft to semi-solid food. Try mixing formula with food when they start eating. Remember to consult with your vet before you change their diet. Also, figure out if you need to give any additional supplements.

- At four to six weeks of age, your puppy should be consuming solid food from a bowl by themselves. Puppy food bags come with recommendations on how much you should feed a puppy. You can follow their measurements to know how much to give per feeding session. A typical feeding schedule for a six to twelve-week-old puppy is four times a day.

BATHROOM CARE

Newborn puppies are not equipped to do their business on their own. Their mothers stimulate their genital and anal areas by licking them. This movement causes the muscles and nerves to become active, leading to the puppy relieving itself. If you are taking care of a newborn puppy without access to their mother, use a gentle washcloth or a cotton ball soaked in lukewarm water and gently stroke the mentioned areas. This simulates their mother's movements and will help them go. This is important because your puppy needs help with bowel movements at this stage.

WHEN SHOULD YOUR PUPPY GO FOR THEIR FIRST VET CHECK-UP?

You should take your puppy for a veterinarian check-up at about six weeks of age. By this time, the mother's antibodies start wearing off, which means they lose protection. This makes them more vulnerable to infections and diseases. During your first visit to the vet, your puppy will get their initial round of immunization and deworming medication. The vaccination for new pups include:

- *Distemper* Virus Vaccination
- *Adenovirus* Vaccination
- *Parainfluenza* Vaccination, and
- *Parvovirus* Vaccination.

Around eight to twelve months, your puppy will require a second round of shots for *Bordetella, Canine Influenza H3N2* and *H3N8, Rabies* Year One, and *Leptospirosis (Caring For a Newborn Puppy, 2021)*.

Don't miss out on regular physical examinations. They will help your vet know whether your puppy is healthy and whether you need to change or adjust your feeding schedule. You'll also know more about their propensity towards certain illnesses or allergies and what you can do to prevent them.

Overall, I would suggest that you do not bring home a puppy younger than two months unless it is unavoidable. All babies require an optimum amount of nutrition and nursing from their mothers. It is our duty to let them have access to this. If we deprive them, it also means that we compromise their health and safety in our haste.

If your situation is dire and the puppy has been abandoned by their mother, or if there is an emergency, don't panic. You will get through it. Remember always to consult your vet for any questions. Before we move on, let's run through what we covered in this chapter.

 **KEY POINTS**

This chapter covers everything you need to know to care for your puppy. You have to treat them as your children by loving and nourishing them. They will return your love ten times over.

Disclaimer: The advice in this section is to aid parents and guardians primarily. You can involve your children in the whole process but stay in the supervisory role.

- Keep a support system around you. Involve everyone close to you, and let them know that you are bringing a new friend into your life.
- Take time and care to proof your house, not just to protect your furniture and valuables but also to keep your puppy from harm.
- Introduce your family members one-by-one. Let your puppy go up to them and sniff them. Only after this, ask each family member to pat and praise them gently.
- Develop a good feeding schedule.
- Be mindful of what not to feed your puppy. Never give them chocolate, sugar, grapes, raisins, caffeine, or dairy.

- Check with a vet to understand if your puppy has any allergies.
- Keep some essentials like bowls, chew toys, bedding, combs, shampoo, collars, and leads in your house.
- Try not to take on a puppy younger than two months.
- If you must take one younger than that, consult with a vet regularly.
- Develop a formula based on the vet's advice.
- Feed a newborn puppy every two to three hours.
- Be on track with their vaccines and immunization schedules.

Caring for a puppy may seem overwhelming when you are starting. This section is meant to serve as a guide for the parents. Of course, your children can and should be involved, but this phase requires medical and technical assistance, which you are equipped to provide.

BONUS DOG TRAINING TIPS

My dear reader, congratulations on coming this far! This truly shows how dedicated you are to your puppy. I am proud of you.

By now, we know that our puppies light up our lives. They are adorable and mischievous, playful, and kind. But, it comes with lots of responsibilities. The initial training phase can take a lot of time and effort. The more of each we invest in our puppy, the stronger our bond becomes with them.

HOW DOES A PUPPY LEARN?

A puppy is trained primarily using two techniques. The first is the *aversive* method, and the second is *reward-based.*

Aversive-based training relies on positive punishment and negative reinforcement techniques. They involve the use of loud, ringing noises, physical correctional methods, and harsh scolding to have your way with your puppy. I am not a fan of this.

The second, the *reward-based* method, uses rewards and positive reinforcement to train your puppy. This style relies on techniques like food luring and gentle, positive encouragement. It believes in treating your puppy with love and patience, as well as using treats and affection to reinforce good behavior.

It is believed that a *reward-based* method sets up a positive relationship of trust between your puppy and you. They learn to associate you with happy feelings and know they will get love and praise when they do what they are told. On the other hand, *aversive-based* training teaches them to fear you. Here, they perform an activity more out of fear of being subject to harsh treatment than out of love.

WHY IS POSiTiVE REiNFORCEMENT IMPORTANT?

Positive reinforcement, or training with rewards, love, and praise, makes the possibility of good behavior likelier. The other thing is- your puppy will be happy. We don't want a sad, frightened pup. We want a loving, energetic one. Positive reinforcement relies on giving your puppy something they like when they behave appropriately, which encourages them to behave this way again.

Training with rewards teaches your puppy that good things result from good discipline and from listening to you. When your puppy earns a reward, they associate this as a prize for what they just did, making them proud and happy. For example, if your puppy gets a treat for sitting, they are likely to do it again.

Positive reinforcement will cement the bond between your puppy and you and allow you to function as a team. Not only will your puppy love you, but they will also respect and look up to you for your instructions.

Most importantly, training with rewards ensures that your puppy develops a healthy dose of self-confidence. This is necessary if you don't want a sad, scared puppy. Puppies need to feel loved and accepted to be confident, so the more you show how proud and happy you are, the better it is for them (*Training with Rewards*: *Positive Reinforcement*, 2021).

UNDERSTANDING YOUR PUPPY'S MIND

A puppy learns a lot like a little child. They don't understand the long-term consequences of their behaviors, and in their head, they are focused on what is happening immediately. Your puppy can understand your mood by your tone, movements, and gestures. That is why it is essential for you to be happy and gentle around them.

Your fur-friend will learn by three processes. *Instinctive learning* happens from birth. They are behaviors that your puppy picks up right from the time they are born, when they spend time with their siblings and their mother. *Adaptive learning* is what your puppy learns from their surroundings and the environment around them. *Working* and *obedience* are the overall sums of the cues they will learn from you (*Dog Training*: *Obedience Training for Dogs*, 2021).

HOW DO YOU PREVENT BAD BEHAVIOR?

When you rely on reward-based training, your puppy needs to understand there will be some consequences for behaving unacceptably. In this case, the consequences will mean withholding the reward if they do something bad.

For example, say your puppy likes to jump and greet you when you come home. You are training them not to do this since it can cause accidents. To achieve success:

1. Do not greet or give them attention if they jump at you.
2. Turn around, go outside, close the door, and come in again.
3. Repeat this till your puppy stops jumping.

As soon as they do, you give them a treat and praise.

All the family members should try this trick till your puppy understands that they cannot jump at people since it means they won't get praise or treats. If you wonder what treats will work best, the simplest thing to do is try a number of them and see which one your puppy likes the most. That will be your high-value treat. As soon as they know a high-value treat is in play, they will do their best to impress you.

This is why positive reinforcement works. You are teaching your puppy without scaring or upsetting them. Here, the puppy is just accepting that to get a treat, they must stop doing something you don't like. This doesn't make them feel sad or depressed; they'll be too busy trying to understand how to impress you to get that treat and some love. When they do, and they get their rewards, it not only makes them happy but also brings them closer to you.

Finally, rely on things that will help you build a relationship of trust with your puppy. That will ensure you grow old together as the best of friends. Believe me; puppies are smart enough to know when you want something from them. So, just like you try to get them to behave, they will also try to test what hold they have over you in the initial phase.

The key is to establish dominance, but gently. You want your puppy to know that you are in a supervisory role, but this is because *you love them, not out of the need to be harsh or angry at them.* When they understand that your commands and cues come from a place of love, trust-building is automatic.

CONCLUSION: THE BEGINNING OF YOUR JOURNEY

Well done! You have reached the end of the book! Now, before you go to begin an incredible journey with your puppy, give me five more minutes of your time.

Make sure you are fully prepared to take on the responsibility of a puppy. Yes, you will gain a lot of love and a lifetime of friendship, but be prepared to return it in equal measure.

Always go through a reputable breeder or a good adoption center. Try to avoid taking on puppies that are too young because they need time to nourish before they come to their forever home.

Get ready for the change that is coming your way. Believe me, your puppy will sweep you off your feet. You will become a more patient, loving, and kinder human. You will learn so much. And most of all, you will earn the trust of an innocent being. There is nothing more precious than that. Here are couple of things to remember.

- Keep a list of emergency contacts ready. Stick them somewhere visible, like on your refrigerator. These should include the number of your vet, your local puppy day-care center, groomers, and anyone else who may be of help.

- When it comes to training your puppy, always remember that it is a two-way street. Work with them as a team. This will not just help your puppy understand you better, it will also make you a better owner.

- The better trained your puppy is, the easier it will be to take them along with you wherever you go. Your puppy will be appreciated for their excellent behavior and discipline, so work toward that.

- The more trained your puppy is, and the more accustomed to voice cues, the better you will be able to protect them when unrestrained. So, a puppy is safer when they know the rules of obedience. They will know when a voice cue means that they are doing something they shouldn't, which is valuable. Trust the process, know that you are working for your puppy's safety and happiness.

- Should you require to be out of the house for a while, a trained puppy will be far more sociable in a boarding facility or with a friend/relative. Otherwise, they will be nervous and anxious and may snap at strangers.

I am glad I got to be a part of your journey. Feel free to wreck my book. Read it as many times as you need to. Make notes, highlight liberally, and mark the pages you need to re-read. This book will take you through all you need to know, from getting your puppy, what games to play, what toys to buy, how to go through housebreaking like a champ, and how to care for your puppy like your own family.

I know it will be hard on occasion. Having a dog has taught me to accept my shortcomings and adjust to them. I have found that being patient has many rewards, and the love of my dog has carried me through so many depressing phases of my life. It is a beautiful feeling to come home from a long day of work or school and be greeted by furry paws. The love and excitement they will show you is a thing to behold, and it can wash away all tiredness or stress. The only things that they ask for in return are love and acceptance.

From my personal experience, having a puppy is a whole lot of teamwork. I had days when I was tired from work, but I always found fifteen minutes to spend time training my puppy. And those fifteen minutes made all the difference. It helped us bond better, it helped my puppy understand what I wanted from them, and most of all, it got me a patient, trained puppy full of confidence and intelligence.

Spending time with your puppy will do your whole family a lot of good. It will reduce stress and promote a happy home environment. Also, did you know that there is scientific research to back your relationship with your puppy? Pet ownership may be beneficial for child and adolescent emotional, behavioral, educational, cognitive, and social development. Young people from pet-loving homes score much higher in cognitive, social, and motor development. There's also proof that having a puppy makes you more empathetic to the needs and emotions of others (Shojai, 2021).

We often talk about a "bond" to describe the love we feel for our puppies. Did you know there is a scientific explanation behind this? Science proves that the effect our puppies have on us results from brain chemicals influencing our thoughts and attitudes. These chemicals lead to feelings of happiness, safety, love, peace, contentment, and elation. This doesn't just happen to you. It affects your puppy in equal measure. So, when bonding takes place, those happy hormones work on both your puppy and you, bringing you together into one wholesome unit (Shojai, 2021).

Finally, your puppy will give you so much exercise. It is especially great if you live a sedentary lifestyle because this will get you moving. The more you move, the more the engagement between the two of you, which will lead to increased happiness. Playing with your puppy can be such a joyful activity. Don't limit it to the insides of your house. There are lots of fun games for the days you don't want to or can't go out, but when you can, play outdoors with them. Your puppy will get much more exercise, and in turn, love you more for your efforts.

So, here we are. I am so proud of you. I am proud that you chose my book, that you took the time to read through it, and plan to take on a family member and a forever friend. This is the start of a new life for you, full of adventure and joy. You are ready to begin your journey. I hope it is full of love and laughter. Welcome to your future.

If you enjoyed my book, I would appreciate it if you could leave a review so others can receive the same benefit as you. It is gratifying for me to know that my work has benefited you, helping me develop further.

PLEASE LEAVE ME A REVIEW!

I would be incredibly thankful if you could take just 60 seconds to write a brief review on Amazon, even if it's just a few sentences!

Customer Reviews

⭐⭐⭐⭐⭐ 2
5.0 out of 5 stars ▾

5 star		100%
4 star		0%
3 star		0%
2 star		0%
1 star		0%

See all verified purchase reviews ›

Share your thoughts with other customers

Write a customer review

A SPECIAL GIFT TO OUR READERS!

Included with your purchase of this book is our **5 Step Challenge** on how to train your dog to roll over. This is a great way to show all your friends and family a neat little trick your fur ball can do.

Included in your 5 Step Challenge is a **checklist** of the most essential things you need for your puppy before it arrives.

Use the Link:
Andrewmalcom.com

Or Scan the QR Code

JOIN OUR ONLINE SUPPORT GROUP

To maximize the value of your training, I highly encourage you to join our tight-knit community on Facebook, where you will be able to ask questions and get tips and tricks.

Use the link:
https://www.facebook.com/groups/puppytrainingcommunity

Or Scan the QR Code

REFERENCES

15 Essential Commands to Teach Your Dog. (2016). InsideDogsWorld. https://www.insidedogsworld.com/essential-commands-to-teach-your-dog/

21 Essential Dog Commands to Teach your Dog. (2020). Gallant. https://www.gallant.com/blog/dog-commands

Basic Dog Training. (2013). Dogs Trust. https://www.dogstrust.org.uk/help-advice/factsheets-downloads/basicdogtrainingfactsheetnov13.pdf%0A%0A

Basic Dogs Training Commands. (2021). Purina. https://www.purina.co.uk/dogs/behaviour-and-training/training-your-dog/basic-commands-for-your-dog

Bringing Home Your New Dog: Preparing And First Steps. (2021). Dog Time. https://dogtime.com/dog-health/general/262-adults-bringing-home

Caring For a New-born Puppy. (2021). Fetch by WebMD. https://pets.webmd.com/dogs/guide/caring-newborn-puppy#3

Common Puppy Training Mistakes New Owners Make! (2020). The Puppy Academy. https://www.thepuppyacademy.com/

blog/2020/1/6/common-puppy-training-mistakes-new-owners-make

Complete Guide For The First Time Puppy Dog Owners. (2021). Time For Paws. https://www.timeforpaws.co.uk/s/Complete-Guide-For-First-Time-Dog-Owners

Conklin, L. M. (2019). *13 Puppy Training Mistakes You'll Regret Later.* Readers' Digest. https://www.rd.com/list/puppy-training-mistakes/

Cooper, W. (2019). *5 Brilliant back garden games your dog will love to play.* Yourbrilliantdog.Com. https://westrow.medium.com/5-brilliant-back-garden-games-your-dog-will-love-to-play-ef444452e059

Dog Temperament Types. (2020). Puppy Play and Stay. https://puppyplayandstay.com/dog-temperament-types/

Dog Training: Obedience Training for Dogs. (2021). Fetch by WebMD. https://pets.webmd.com/dogs/guide/dog-training-obedience-training-for-dogs#1

Dog Training. (2021). RSPCA. https://www.rspca.org.uk/adviceandwelfare/pets/dogs/training/

Duno, S. (2021). *Are You Making These Puppy Training Mistakes?* Modern Dog. https://moderndogmagazine.com/puppytraining

Essential equipment for your puppy or dog. (2021). The Kennel Club. https://www.thekennelclub.org.uk/getting-a-dog/buying-a-dog/essential-equipment-for-your-puppy-or-dog/

Garden dog toys. (2018). Purina. https://www.purina.co.uk/dog/bakersdogfood/dog-fun/garden-dog-toys

Harris, S. (2021). *My Puppy Pees A Lot.... Why?* AdvidPup. https://www.dailydogstuff.com/puppy-pees-a-lot/

Horwitz, D. (2021). *Puppy Behavior and Training - Training Basics.* VCA. https://vcahospitals.com/know-your-pet/puppy-behavior-and-training-training-basics

House Training Your Puppy. (2021). Fetch by WebMD. https://pets.webmd.com/dogs/guide/house-training-your-puppy#1

How To Crate Train Your Dog. (2021). The People's Dispensary for Sick Animals. https://www.pdsa.org.uk/taking-care-of-your-pet/looking-after-your-pet/puppies-dogs/crate-training

How to Create a DIY Agility Course in Your Backyard. (2020). Nutri Source. https://nutrisourcepetfoods.com/blog/pet-parents/how-to-create-a-diy-agility-course-in-your-backyard/

How To Teach A Dog Its Name. (2021). BatterSea. https://www.battersea.org.uk/pet-advice/dog-care-advice/how-teach-dog-its-name

Lunchick, P. (2021). *Teach Your Puppy These 5 Basic Cues.* American Kennel Club. https://www.akc.org/expert-advice/training/teach-your-puppy-these-5-basic-commands/

Mckeeby, C. (2018). *How to Take Care of a Puppy: A New Owner's Guide.* Care.Com. https://www.care.com/c/stories/15173/how-to-take-care-of-a-puppy-a-new-owners-guide/

Mixed or Purebred Puppy: Which is Better? (2017). PetMD Editorial. https://www.petmd.com/dog/puppycenter/adoption/evr_dg_mixed_or_purebred_puppy_which_is_better

Mouthing, Nipping and Biting in Puppies. (2021). ASPCA. https:// www.aspca.org/pet-care/dog-care/common-dog-behavior-issues/mouthing-nipping-and-biting-puppies#:~:text=Most puppy mouthing is normal, signal problems with future aggression.&text=Puppies sometimes have temper tantrums, something he doesn't like.

Outdoor Games You Can Play With Your Puppy. (2021). Keystone Puppies. https://www.keystonepuppies.com/blog/activities/outdoor-games-can-play-puppy

Puppy House Training. (2021). Royal Canin. https://www.royalcanin.com/uk/dogs/puppy/puppy-training-and-play/puppy-house-training?gclid=EAIaIQobChMIIaCHoOvi7gIVI4BQBh2BRg-4EAAYAiAAEgI78_D_BwE&gclsrc=aw.ds

Puppy Training Advice and Tips. (2021). Purina. https://www.purina.co.uk/dogs/key-life-stages/puppies/training-your-puppy

Schade, V. (2017). *10 Potty Training Mistakes You're Probably Making.* PawCulture.

Shojai, A. (2021). *5 Reasons Puppies Are Good For Us.* The Spruce Pets. https://www.thesprucepets.com/health-benefits-of-puppies

Shore, J. (2020). *How To Teach A Puppy Their Name – And How You Should Use It.* Labrador Training HQ. https://www.labradortraininghq.com/labrador-training/how-to-teach-a-puppy-its-name/

Stregowski, J. (n.d.). *10 Common Dog Training Mistakes.* The Spruce Pets. Retrieved March 29, 2021, from https://www.thesprucepets.com/common-dog-training-mistakes-4030442

Stregowski, J. (2020). *Puppies 101: How to Care for a Puppy*. The Spruce Pets. https://www.thesprucepets.com/how-to-care-for-puppies-1117475

Stuck inside with your pet due to coronavirus? Try these indoor games for dogs. (2021). Blue Cross for Pets. https://www.bluecross.org.uk/pet-advice/coronavirus-indoor-dog-games

Toilet Training a Puppy. (2021). Blue Cross for Pets. https://www.bluecross.org.uk/pet-advice/toilet-training-puppy

Training with rewards: Positive Reinforcement. (2021). DogTrust. https://www.dogstrust.org.uk/help-advice/training/positive-reinforcement-training-with-rewards

Wall, J. (2021). *27 Dog Tricks You Can Teach Your Pup Right Now*. Love Your Dog. https://www.loveyourdog.com/tricks/%0A%0A

Welton, M. (2021). *Puppy Training Schedule: What to Teach Puppies, and When*. Your Purebred Puppy. https://www.yourpurebredpuppy.com/training/articles/puppy-training-schedule.html

What is Puppy Socialization. (2021). The Kennel Club. https://www.thekennelclub.org.uk/getting-a-dog/caring-for-your-new-puppy/what-is-puppy-socialisation/

Dog Temperament Types. (2020). Puppy Play and Stay. https://puppyplayandstay.com/dog-temperament-types/

How to Create a DIY Agility Course in Your Backyard. (2020). Nutri Source. https://nutrisourcepetfoods.com/blog/pet-parents/how-to-create-a-diy-agility-course-in-your-backyard/

Mixed or Purebred Puppy: Which is Better? (2017). PetMD Editorial. https://www.petmd.com/dog/puppycenter/adoption/ evr_dg_mixed_or_purebred_puppy_which_is_better

Outdoor Games You Can Play With Your Puppy. (2021). Keystone Puppies. https://www.keystonepuppies.com/blog/activities/ outdoor-games-can-play-puppy

Why Playtime Is of the Utmost Importance for Your Dog. (2021). Scottsdale Pet Hotel. https://www.scottsdalepethotel.com/ importance-playtime-dogs/

Zebib, R. (2013). *33 Simple Ways to Keep Your Dog Busy Indoors.* Puppy Leaks. https://www.puppyleaks.com/ easy-ways-to-keep-your-dog-busy-indoors/

Printed in Great Britain
by Amazon

74850847R00106